The Passion of Jesus

by Lauri Matisse

The Passion of Jesus

The Passion of Jesus

I was thinking of you…

by Lauri Matisse

Published by Matisse Studios, Fayetteville, Arkansas

Printed and bound in the United States of America

ISBN 978-09630069-6-7

Library of Congress #2017910822

Other books by Lauri Matisse:

Eve's Memoirs ISBN 978-0-9630069-5-0
Eve's Diary from the 100th year of the Dawn $12.95

no more black days: ISBN 0-9630069-1-6
Complete Freedom from Eating Disorders and Other Compulsive Behaviors
New Version: **no more dark days:** ISBN: 9781097770922

The Walking Dead: ISBN 0-9630069-3-2; New Version: 9781690822141
Information for the Information Age of Ignorance $13.00

To order books please visit: www.EvesMemoirs.com
Lauri's Blog: *Weaving Light* — laurimatisseblog.wordpress.com
www.LauriMatisse.com   www.matissestudios.com
https://www.patreon.com/LauriMatisse

Special Thanks

Jamie Chandler-Developmental Editor

Bunni Slater- Proofreading and Encouragement

My wonderful and supportive friends and family

The Passion of Jesus

I was thinking of you…

An Intimate Journey with Jesus
from Gethsemane to Calvary

Originally broadcast as a radio show called *The Breath of God* which aired
on Trinity Broadcast Network and shortwave radio to the Middle East

From the Author:

Having read the bible hundreds of times and spent much of my life in prayer, I've attempted, with humility, in this book, to offer an in-depth insight into the devotion Jesus has for the world.

"For God so loved the world, that He sent His only Son,
That through Him, we might be saved." John 3:16

Many of Jesus' thoughts, I have written in this book, are not His words verbatim, but paraphrased from scriptures with an artistic license to imagine what His thoughts may have been. Although the artistic license of these thoughts exhibit what I feel to be in line with the Word and the character of Jesus, unless it is a direct quote or paraphrased verse quoted, they are just my thoughts laced with scripture.

Each chapter focuses on a main passage of scripture. The verses cited at the beginning of each chapter are interwoven throughout the chapter but not always cited directly in the chapter.

Most of the scriptures directly quoted or slightly paraphrased are in *italics* throughout the book. Some others are referenced and put in quotation marks, but the reader should keep in mind the entire book is scripturally based. Satan has not been capitalized on purpose, except at the beginning of a sentence.

I hope each reader finds a deeper understanding of what our Savior experienced historically, as well as gains a more intimate insight to His love for humanity.

Since our gospel is to be *"to the Jew first, then the Gentile,"* I have inserted words in Hebrew (*in italics*) and have presented nuggets of facts regarding the history of the roots of our faith in Israel as much as possible. If there are errors or omissions, they have not been done intentionally.

The chapters are laid out in scenes, much like the scene of a movie. During each scene the reader is brought *into* the scene *with Jesus* as He experiences that moment of the journey to the cross, at the same time, He projects His thoughts and feelings for you, here and now, *"I was thinking of you...'*

The Passion of Jesus, written as a dramatic ready for a radio show, was written to be read aloud and I encourage you to do so, or listen to the audible version.

Although I grew up Christian, I suffered from eating disorders and severe depression. When I was 23, I called out to Jesus. A supernatural breath sucked demonic creatures off of my body. I was healed and filled with joy.

Soon after this ecstatic experience, I was listening to a radio show in Santa Monica, California. I remember the exact location on Pico Blvd. near the Pacific Ocean. The commentator on the radio was describing the crucifixion of Jesus in detail.

It was at the moment the story of Jesus' death because intensely personal. I *knew* he had died for me and that my sin was nailed to Him on the cross. These two experiences being the most pivotal of my life, I have endeavored to write, speak, create, all of my life's works to give glory and honor to Him whom honor is due.

I vowed I would have a radio show one day to share this message of the crucifixion of Messiah Jesus. I started writing this book, I *was Thinking of you...* as a dramatical reading which broadcast for two years on TBN and on shortwave to the Middle East.

Many listeners wanted me to write the work into a book, but I could not finish the book. I simply could not finish the chapters of His actually death on the cross. It took 17 years and much suffering for Him, before I could finish the book.

I hope you will find a more intimate walk with Him as you read *The Passion of Jesus* and share this work with others who don't yet know Him. I am also praying for the book to be translated into other languages and be able to have books available for those who need one for free.

—If you would like to be involved or support my work to do this, please contact me. Information is at the end of the book.

"In The Passion of Jesus,
Lauri Matisse weaves together historical fact
with imaginative insight
regarding Jesus' thoughts
of devotion for those He loves,
as He journeys
From Gethsemane to Calvary."

I live to weave
The thread of redemption
Through the complex journey
Of the human soul

Lauri Matisse

How precious also are Your thoughts to me, O God!
How great is the sum of them!
If I should count them, they would be more in number than the sand;
When I awake, I am still with You.
Psalm 139:17-18

Setting...
The Mount of Olives

Luke 22:39-52

The full moon lit up the long ridge paralleling the eastern part of Jerusalem—in the Garden of Gethsemane, as I knelt beside a rock, all alone, praying and thinking of you...

My disciples were a stone's throw away—*sleeping*.

Only a few short moments ago, just before twilight, the pink glow of the sunset cast a flickering radiance on My people of Israel who had begun to make preparations for the *Pesach*—the sacred Passover feast which they celebrated once a year to remind them of their miraculous exodus from slavery in Egypt.

With My head bowed solemnly, I contemplated the arduous path I would walk before the lambs would be slaughtered tomorrow at three o'clock in the afternoon—less than 24 hours from now.

I had just finished eating the last supper with My disciples. In this final, precious time together with them, I had attempted to etch an image into their minds regarding the events that would follow. I knew they could not fathom what I meant when I said...

"With desire I have desired to eat this passover with you before I suffer:
For I say to you, I will not eat anymore,
Until it be fulfilled in the kingdom of God."
Luke 22:15-16

As I washed each of their feet, one by one, I took note of their bewildered faces. Each of these men, except one, would understand later, what I meant when I explained the actions of a true servant...

"The greatest among you will be a servant of all."

Each of their precious feet will walk boldly after My death and resurrection, spreading the good news of My salvation, but I knew as I expounded on the events to come, they were not fully aware of My

17

Father's plan, just as many of their contemporaries did not understand the first coming of their Messiah.

I knew that tonight would change their lives forever.

As they squabbled among themselves about who would be the greatest in the kingdom of heaven, I spoke the words that sliced the air like a knife…

"Truly, one of you will betray Me."

My disciples were very sorrowful when they heard this and discussed among themselves whom it might be. The twelve were very close. "How could it be any of them?" they wondered.

I caught Judas' eye as he dipped his bread into the cup. I knew what he would do. He knew what he would do. He had already chosen the crooked path that lay ahead of him this night.

"Woe to the man by whom the Son of man is betrayed.
It would have been better for that man if he had not been born."

I felt sad for Judas as I spoke these words, but I knew his actions would not be altered. He had made his decision. I would now need to focus on My decision—a decision which held more weight than his—more weight than any human could ever imagine.

During the dinner, I felt so close to My beloved disciples, Peter, James and John, who sat so very near Me, hanging on every word I spoke. As I broke the bread, I wished this time of fellowship would last forever. In one sense, it would last forever, as I was to become the Bread of eternal life.

"Take it and eat. This is My body given for you.
As often as you eat, remember Me."
Luke 22:19

As the disciples passed the bread around the table, I was certain My sincere followers did not understand what I meant. How could they? The ways of My Father in heaven are much higher than the ways of man. His thoughts are much higher than their thoughts.

I took the cup of wine and gave thanks to My Father in Heaven…
"This cup is My blood of the covenant between Yahuweh and His people,
Which is poured out for you and for the world.
Truly, I will not drink again from the fruit of the vine,
Until that day when I drink it new in the Kingdom of God."
Luke 22:20

Even though we sang a psalm together after the supper was over, I could not shake the heaviness in My spirit, as we had headed toward the Mount of Olives. I wished the feasting with My loved ones could have lasted all night, but alas, I knew what lay ahead. I knew what I must do. I would become the Feast of Israel.

I had prophesied to them that they would all will fall away because of what I must go through tonight...

"This very night you will all fall away on account of Me.
For it is written: 'I will strike the shepherd,
And the sheep of the flock will be scattered.'"
Matthew 26:31

Peter, determined to be steadfast to the end, had quickly declared... *"Though they fall away because of You, I will never fall away!"*

Although I appreciated his bravery, I was deeply acquainted with his secret heart, as well as his innermost thoughts. This gregarious fisherman, who had become one of My first disciples, was physically strong and willing, but the strength that would be required this night would not be one of the body; the strength tonight would be one of the soul. Peter, who had been called Simon, would emerge as the rock on which I will build my church, but not until he had endured a great trial.

He did not understand when I said to him...

"Simon, Simon, satan has asked to sift all of you as wheat, but I
have prayed for you, Simon, that your faith may not fail. And when you
have turned back, strengthen your brothers."

Peter replied, "Lord, I am ready to go with you to prison and to death." But I answered firmly...

"I tell you, Peter, before the rooster crows today, you will deny
three times that you know Me."
Luke 22:31-32-34

The time had come for the Son of Man to be lifted up.

As we continued our journey to the Garden, also called, "The Oil Press," on the lower slope of the Mount of Olives, the golden lantern moon cast a shadow of My body onto the hillside. It was a long shadow—a looming shadow—a shadow of death.

I reflected on David's twenty-third psalm.

"As I walk through the shadow of death, I will fear no evil."

This comforted My soul.

I thought of My disciples' faces before we parted, as they questioned Me with their eyes full of wonder. I returned their gaze, looking deeply into each of their souls. They might have thought I would overthrow the Roman Government in a few days. They might have been asking themselves if they had the courage to fight for My Kingdom. Possibilities and scenarios of the events to come, crowded their minds, but I had already spoken.

As I soberly left to pray, I asked them to join me...

"Stay with Me and keep watch with Me."

But alas, they were very sleepy.

I had to keep alert. It was vital for Me to keep watch. I watched and prayed, for after all, I knew what I must do.

As I began to pray, I did not notice the beauty of the moon's shadows playing softly on the branches of the olive trees, for all the while, I was thinking of you. My soul was sorrowful, even to the point of death.

My knees began to ache for I had been here quite some time. Tears began to fall as I prayed for you. The tears felt heavy. Each tear seemed to represent one soul, each precious human soul, of every generation, who depended on Me at this moment to make the decision that would save their life forever.

Great drops of thick, red blood began to fall down my face. I had never sweated drops of blood before. I asked My Father in heaven if there was any other way, for I knew the decision I had to make. I was thinking of you, as well as all of humanity, hanging in the balances between heaven and hell. I was fully aware of the cup that was set before Me. I knew the liquid I must drink, the liquid of My Father's perfect judgment, the price of redemption. The cup contained the bride price for each soul. The Father's price for his beloved people would require a blood sacrifice. The cup I must accept is the will of the Father.

The cup contained molecules of you, your life, your decisions, your sin, your death, but more importantly—your inherent need for atonement. The cup held the Garden of Eden, the fall of humanity, the sins of Adam and Eve, as well as the sins of every person who had ever lived, who was living now, or will live on the earth after tonight. The cup held the solemn words—No other way, but His way—the perfect way; the Way, the Truth and the Life of Me—Messiah Jesus.

If I died for many, the way would be complete. I contemplated the way which would be paved in My blood, as I prayed and wept...

"Father, if it is possible... if there is any other way...
Let this cup pass from before Me..."

I tasted blood on my lips and tongue as the drops of blood streamed down my face into my mouth—only a foretaste of what was to come. I heard a band of soldiers approaching in the distance. I could hear their angry voices, but they faded from view for, after all, I was thinking of you...

Small rocks were now embedded in my knees, my stiff shoulders drooped. My head throbbed. The blood seeping from My pores had soaked My robe. I knew what lay before Me this night and the next day. The road stretched into eternity. Planned many yesterdays ago, unto countless tomorrows—the scarlet thread of redemption was woven into these words I would utter with great effort—an effort that echoed the Grace of God throughout all time.

I saw My Father in Heaven. I sensed His Heart beating for you. I felt His Love for you as He longed for you to be near Him—to be close to Him—to be in fellowship with Him forever—never again to be separated from Him. For if you have seen Me, Jesus, the Messiah, you have seen the Father's love poured out for you. I am the face of *Yahuweh*.

I pictured My Father's heart breaking for you and weeping for you, as My heart had wept just moments before. My heart beat in rhythm with His heart—for I and the Father are One. As One, we created the heavens and the earth. As One, We breathed our Holy Breath, the *Ruach HuKodesh*, over the face of the waters.

As One God, *Elohim*, Father, Son and Spirit, move with compassion tonight in the Garden. Together, though separate—loving, breathing, sacrificing—for you. The Father giving the Son; the Son giving His life; the Spirit comforting your soul as you feel comforted now, so you may be together with the Father, the Son and the Spirit forever.

Elohim, the plurality of God in One, who holds the universe in the span of His hand, created the beginning and the end. In Elohim was the Word, Me, the Messiah. The Word was *with Elohim*, and the Word *was Elohim*. The Word, your Messiah, made all things. I had become flesh and lived among the people on Earth now for 33 years. With the heart of God, but with the flesh of a very tender man, I knew it was time to finish the

21

work that I came here to do. I would accomplish My Father's will, to be the Savior of the world, *Yeshua of Yahuweh.*

I saw you in the distance, not yet born. I was thinking of you, as I am thinking of you now. I did not have to drink the cup. I did not have to make the choice. I was God after all; yet all the while, I was thinking of you...

My Father in Heaven sent an angel to strengthen Me. The angel of the Lord laid an unseen hand on my shoulder. I could feel the warmth of His presence. One day, when you feel utterly exhausted, when your heart is in severe pain, pouring out blood mixed with tears, in your garden of decision, My Father will send an angel to strengthen you; for after all, He is thinking of you.

I lifted My weary body. This poignant time of prayer was My last moment of freedom I would experience before My crucifixion. I looked over at the bodies of those who had said they would always stand by me. I asked them why they were sleeping—for they ought to be praying —in case a time of great testing came upon them, a time to try their faith, to see if it was pure, made of gold, to see if heaven was their goal or if earthly desires were their aim. Many of My followers throughout the centuries would hear My same plea, "Watch and pray." Many would sleep as well, for the spirit is willing, but the flesh is weak

I was alone then and would be alone now until the end, which is really the beginning, as I accomplish My purpose on this earth. All the while, thinking of you...

"Wake up, disciples! I said to Peter, James and John.
Look! The time has come.
The Son of Man is betrayed into the hands of sinners."

The Roman soldiers came with swords and clubs with which to take Me by force. They appeared along with the Scribes and Pharisees, who taught the *Torah* daily in the temple of Jerusalem. Bursting onto our humble scene with great force and fleshly might, they shouted, "Where Is this Jesus of Nazareth who calls himself, the Messiah?"

Judas, who was among them, greeted Me with a kiss. "Rabbi, *Shalom!*" he cried out loudly, "Rabbi! Teacher! The One we followed!" His nervousness must have caused him to raise his voice louder in an attempt to drown out his wretched decision he made only a few days before—his decision to betray Me, his Lord, his Messiah. He had one eye on Me and the other on the soldiers. A double-minded man is unstable in all his ways. Judas, with his divided heart, teetered on a very jagged ledge.

Judas, my good friend, my follower, was not an enemy. If he were, I could have borne the betrayal much easier. He was one who took great interest in Me and My ministry. He sat very near Me, kept My accounts and records, so that I would not become burdened with shekels or coins of Caesar. He, however, became very burdened with coins. Thirty pieces of silver caused him to betray Me, His Lord. That is why it is so important to serve God and not money; one becomes enslaved to one and hates the other. Judas—hatred ingrained in his heart, or perhaps fear, which coupled with hatred proves to be a fatally flawed combination—had betrayed Me.

We had taken sweet counsel together over the past three years through the Galilean countryside. We had worshipped in the temple. In love and purity, we had fellowship as we fed the 5,000. When he approached Me, I looked at him with eyes of love that seemed to pierce his soul. I was not condemning him. I loved him. He was one of My own dearly beloved twelve. With the mind of a man, I hoped that even now he would turn from his destiny of destruction and run away, but with the heart of God, I knew his decision was cast long ago. Judas had condemned himself, and it grieved me so.

I kept staring at him—in this moment, frozen in time, but he would not look at Me. He cast his eyes to the ground and quickly turned away. I could smell the sweat of his brow. It was not the same smell of perspiration, I had experienced in the garden, where I had just prayed, the sweat of self-sacrifice. No, it was the haunting, bone-chilling, clammy sweat of guilt running down his face and his hands. Even though he wiped his palms together many times, he could not shake the perspiration nor the chill...

You might know the feeling—impending doom with no escape, when you have done exactly as you planned only to find out your plans are perspiring with perversion. You are enslaved to your desires, cursing the coins you once counted, as you perish in a field of blood, hanging by your own device...

But Judas was not thinking of this. He had stopped thinking. If only he had returned My gaze, perhaps He could have found forgiveness in My eyes, for I came to die for all men and women. All who look on Me with a humble heart can enter into My grace. But as he slithered away as a snake, crawling on his belly through the grass, I said,

"Oh Judas, do you betray Me with a kiss?"

To be betrayed by a friend is the worst betrayal of all. I could have stopped him, but I was not thinking of him any longer, I was thinking of you... The day you would be betrayed by the one that you loved. When someone you trusted, someone with whom you were deeply intimate with, orders a secret council to lynch you behind your back, in order to accuse you of wrongdoings you have not done—in an attempt to sell you in exchange for someone else—you can be comforted in the fact that I, too, was betrayed. I know how you feel.

If you, by your selfish desires, are the one who has betrayed someone you love, don't run away...

Stop, lift your eyes and look at Me. I am thinking of you, and my eyes are full of forgiveness, of compassion, of love. You can be forgiven, even now. I am thinking of you.

I am Jesus, your Messiah, your great High Priest, your advocate, who stands at the right hand of the Father in heaven, making intercession for you daily. Hold firmly to your faith in times of trouble, for you do not have a priest, a rabbi, or a Lord who does not feel your weaknesses. Your Messiah has experienced the depth of every person's feelings. In all points, I was tempted as you are, yet I was and am without sin. Because of this, you can come boldly to the throne of God to obtain mercy. Come. You will find grace in your time of need. *Hebrews 4:15-16*

When you need Me, you have a God who had become a man so that you, as a man, woman or child, could have access to *Yahuweh* by Grace. It is for this reason, tonight, in the Garden, I am willing to lay down my life.

For *you*, I was able to utter the words to My Father...
"Not *My* will but *Thine*, be done."

For I was thinking of you, as I am thinking of you now...

24

Setting...
The Mount of Olives

John 18:1-14; John 17

My followers were furious at this attempt to arrest Me. Peter drew his sword quickly. In his valiant attempt to protect me, he cut off the right ear of Malchus, a servant. Blood gushed from wounded Malchus. The soldiers and guards flashed their swords in a split second, but even before they could retaliate, I touched Malchus and healed his ear...

"My kingdom is not of this earth,"

I prompted Peter to put away his sword, and reminded My disciples My Kingdom is *not* of this earth...

"If My kingdom were of this earth...

I would have my servants fight."

The only blood I desired to be shed tonight was my own. Peter, Malchus, the Roman guards, the chief priests and Scribes did not know what they were doing, just as you might not know what you are doing one day, many years from now, when you are unaware that My kingdom is not of this earth. Spiritual warfare is not a battle of flesh and blood. The Kingdom of God will never be a kingdom on the earth. The real Kingdom is made up of souls who worship Me in spirit and in truth—those who know Me and recognize who I am.

The religious leaders, eager to bring Me before their council, viscously examined Me with their gaze. They had their cushy lives in the synagogue, and I proposed a threat to their comfort, as well as their authority, even though it is Me whom they have been waiting for. They are not unlike some of you, the times when you realize that if I am truly the Messiah, the anointed One of God, I might interfere with your plans, your dreams, your position in society or work, or even your religious profession.

I said to the hostile group of men swarming around Me...

"Have you come out with swords and clubs to arrest Me,

As you would a robber?

Every day I was with you in the temple teaching,

And you did not capture Me."

I knew, of course, this was happening to fulfill the scriptures. If the religious leaders had *known* the Father, they would have known Me. They would have recognized Me as their Messiah, but alas, those at the top of an organized religion, have often lost their zeal. Perhaps when they were children, they looked up, waited and longed for their Messiah to come, but now as I stood before them, their eyes had become so blind with rules and they had become so accustomed to their own power, they could not see the King of the Universe standing three feet in front of them. The sense of their own power deluded them, so they could not witness My power.

I wished for their sakes they could remember their pure hearts as children...

"Assuredly, I say to you, unless you are converted and become as little children, you will by no means enter the kingdom of heaven. Therefore whoever humbles himself as this little child is the greatest in the kingdom of heaven." Matthew 18:2-4

The guards positioned themselves to seize Me. At that precise second, I could have called upon legions of angels to prove My identity, surround the men with flaming swords and eyes full of fire, but no, that is not how this story would go. I had to let the wicked band take me, because I was thinking of you...

I was thinking of the day your heart may have become so hard and your eyes so blind, when the child of your heart is long since buried in the past. You might even accuse Me and take Me to trial in your court. You may question Me and demand a response and not be satisfied with My answer. Perhaps you will accuse Me without solid evidence or criticize My followers.

If you misunderstand Me or follow someone else's misguided orders down a seductive path of organizational rules which teeter toward the point of ridiculousness—it is at that moment, you will need a Redeemer. As stated in the law...

"Without the shedding of blood, there is no remission of sins."

For as it is stated in Leviticus 17:11, the life is in the blood, and I will give My blood in order to make atonement for anyone who calls on My name.

"For in Me is life, and the life is the Light of all humankind."
John 1:4

A day of atonement cannot take the place of the blood sacrifice. In a very short time after tonight, there will be no temple in Jerusalem anymore. The walls of the temple will crumble to the ground, but as I prophesied...

My blood will be shed tonight, I will become the Temple, because I am thinking of you...

Rules, religion, and temple liturgy, steeped in the traditions of men can keep you from *knowing* Me. On the Mount of Olives, I reflected on the people I had encountered over the past three years. Most of them did not recognize Me, even though they had been waiting for Me, for thousands of years. The prophet Isaiah prophesied that I would be despised and rejected of men, but My people did not listen to Isaiah. He had been brushed aside as prophets typically are throughout the centuries or stoned to death.

The chief Scribes and priests exalted their rituals, such as the washing of hands, more important than the words of Isaiah when he wrote...

"Who hath believed our report?
And to whom is the arm of the Lord revealed?
For He shall grow up before him as a tender plant,
And as a root out of a dry ground:
He hath no form nor comeliness; and when we shall see Him,
There is no beauty that we should desire Him.
He is despised and rejected of men; a man of sorrows,
And acquainted with grief: and we hid as it were our faces from Him;
He was despised, and we esteemed Him not.
Surely He hath borne our griefs, and carried our sorrows:
Yet we did esteem Him stricken, smitten of God, and afflicted.
But He was wounded for our transgressions,
He was bruised for our iniquities:
The chastisement of our peace was upon Him;
And with His stripes we are healed.
All we like sheep have gone astray;
We have turned every one to his own way;
And the Lord hath laid on Him the iniquity of us all.
He was oppressed, and he was afflicted,

*Yet He opened not His mouth: He is brought as a lamb to the slaughter,
and as a sheep before her shearers is dumb, so He opened not his mouth."*
Isaiah 53

These teachers of the *Torah* worshipped their own righteousness rather than their very own Messiah who stood before them. Years from now, they will do the same. Parts of the book of Isaiah will never be read in the synagogues for two thousand years to come, because they will point so clearly to Me, or they will be interpreted by there being two Messiahs — a suffering Messiah and a reigning Messiah. It is the scriptures who speak of Me.

*"Search the scriptures for in them,
You think you have eternal life: and the scriptures testify of Me."*
John 5:39

The Scribes and the Pharisees, the leaders of the temple, the keepers of the *Torah*, with their rabbinical laws did not understand *ME*, just as you might not understand Me. Your religious rules will so often blind you from the Truth. When you burn incense, wear priestly robes, or offer praise from your lips, your heart may be very far from Me.

You might rest on *Shabbat*. You may go to temple and pray. You might attend mass each Sunday morning or follow a tradition, but will forget to *hear* My words. I have asked my followers to give up their own life...

*"If you lose your life, you will find it.
Whoever loses his life for My sake will find it."*

You see — a religious person may appear to be wise, even appear to be good — but *Yahuweh* looks at the *hearts* of men and women. I did not see suits of armor or priestly robes surrounding Me, during of My arrest. No, I observed the hearts of men — some in confusion, wondering why they had come to arrest such a gentle man; some in doubt, such as Judas, wondering if he had done the right thing; and some, such as the Scribes and Pharisees, were filled with hate and fear, with hearts as stony as the rocky ground I had just knelt upon to pray.

I was contemplating their hearts, just as I was thinking of your heart. True religion is in the heart, and I am seeking to build a kingdom of hearts. Anyone can look good on the outside, but God sees on the inside. Just as God spoke to Samuel the prophet when he was looking for the next king. Samuel examined each of Jesse's seven sons, but each one did not make the cut in God's eyes. Samuel was looking at their physical strength and stature, when My Father said to him...

"Do not look at his appearance or at the height of his stature, Because I have rejected him; for God sees not as man sees, for man looks at the outward appearance, but the Lord looks at the heart."

I Samuel 16:7

God singled out David, the youngest brother, who was out tending the sheep. God had noticed David's heart. He knew he was the one who would valiantly slay the giant, Goliath, and later become the renowned king of Israel

"Before Abraham was, I am."

I had said this to the teachers of the *Torah*. I was standing before them—their Messiah, their Lord—yet they did not recognize Me, because they were not looking for the *heart* of God. They were looking for a distinguished ruler on earth who would give them more power and stature —someone prestigious, prominent, and esteemed in *their* eyes—someone to overthrow the Roman government. They did not remember the words of King David who prophesied of Me...

"I am a worm, scorned by men and despised by the people..."

Psalm 22

The religious leaders so often would rather follow religious rules than be in a relationship with the very God who made the rules.

"I have not come to abolish the Law, but to fulfill it."

Matthew 5:17

In refusing to accept their Messiah, they exchange the righteousness of God for their own self-righteousness. It is for this reason, I must die, for even the best of the best cannot keep the rules. My rules demand perfection. If there is not perfection, then the Law requires a perfect blood sacrifice, a spotless lamb.

Even though the religious leaders could not understand Me, even though they did not receive Me, I did not hate them. I loved them. I came for My own—the lost sheep of the house of Israel. The children of Israel were My first-born son. Though they forget Me, I will not forget them...

"I have engraved them on the palms of My hands."

Isaiah 49:16

Some of My people of Israel *did,* however, recognize Me and receive Me, such as My disciples, Lazarus, Mary and Martha, Mary Magdalene, Mary, My mother, and her sister. Throughout the rest of history, there will be those who take up their own cross and follow Me for it is written...

"You must take up your cross and follow Me."

Mark:34

Yet, many people throughout the rest of history will claim that I am a teacher, a rabbi, a zealot from Nazareth or even a prophet from God, but each of these well-meaning persons will fail to believe My Word and what I truly have taught. What I prophesied in the Word was Myself. I Am the fulfillment of the prophecies in the *Tanakh*—they point to Me.

Many times over the past three years, the religious leaders of the Temple had taken up stones to throw at Me. They even disclosed their desire to toss Me over a hill headlong. Many times, I hid Myself from them, passing through the crowd unnoticed. The timing of these incidents were in My control. It was not My time to die. My life or My death is not now, nor has ever been, in the hands of men.

Now, however, the time had come—the time appointed for the hour of darkness. The time had come for Me to die.

As I prayed My fervent prayer to My Father in Heaven, a few days before, I was thinking of My disciples and I was thinking of you...

"Father, the hour has come for Me to be delivered into the power of darkness..."

I was ready to face this darkness for your sake, so when you are in your darkest hour, you will know that your Messiah, your Savior, entered into darkness to overcome darkness with Light...

"Father... glorify your Son, so that the Son may glorify You,
Just as You have given Him authority over all mankind,
So that He might give eternal life
To all those whom you have given Him..."

John 17

I was thinking of you, as I am thinking of you now...

The day when you would realize your own shortcomings, your weaknesses, and your sins—when you might have lied, cheated, murdered, committed adultery, fornication, gossiped, or even hated your brother, which to Me is the same as murder—when you may have used people for your own gain or left a wounded man by the side of the road or discriminated against someone when they did not share the same color of skin or believe in your religion.

I was thinking of the day when your guilt would be eating away inside of you and no matter how many times you cleaned your cup, washed your hands or confessed your sin, you would still feel the need to be washed in your heart.

The sheer discovery of your *own* nakedness, when you fall on your knees, trembling with fear—when you realize there is, in fact, a Judgment Day, and you will be judged by a perfect Judge. The day you realize that if you stood before this perfect Judge, you would be found guilty, when even your good works will unravel in the light of His Presence. Your inner motives and the secrets of your heart are revealed and your face is pressed into the cold hard ground waiting for the hammer of Judgment to fall—it is then—I am thinking of you...

It is for you I will walk through this Judgment—the proverbial hammer will fall on My head instead. When the light shines on your imperfections and weaknesses, and you realize you need a ransom for your sin, I must finish the work I was sent to do—to die in your place so that you can live...

"...For the penalty of sin is death, but the gift of God is eternal life through Me, the righteous Messiah."

Romans 6:23

As I finished My prayer as I gazed into heaven...

"Father, the time has come, glorify Your Son."

The Roman soldiers, some of the largest and strongest specimens of manhood who I had created, now surrounded Me. The officials from the chief priests and Scribes of the temple, carrying torches, lanterns and weapons, pressed in and asked for Jesus of Nazareth.

I answered, *"I Am He."*

As I uttered these three simple words, the men all fell backward to the ground. For one ordained moment, they were utterly humbled by the in the presence of the One True and Living God.

Although the moment was truly radiant, tonight at the Mount of Olives, is not My time to be revered and celebrated. It is My time to bear the sins of the whole world. To take upon Myself the ugliness of the shortcomings of humankind—to be like a Lamb led to the slaughter—so

31

that on the day of your personal visitation from God, and you hear the words, *"I am He," and you fall to the ground*—when you are without excuse—in My name, Jesus, you can be excused, pardoned and ransomed, once and for all.

Look at Me. I am looking with eyes of love and forgiveness. I will go willingly with My enemies tonight, for after all, I was thinking of you, as I am thinking of you now...

I said to My perpetrators, as I held out My hands for them to arrest Me—

"Shall I not drink of the cup the Father has given Me?"

Setting...
En Route to Jerusalem for the Trial before Anais, Caiaphas, and the Sanhedrin

Mark 14:12-51

The world's thoughts of glory and My thoughts of glory are very different. The world looks at splendor, wealth, riches and honor in this life. The path to the glory of God is filled with self-sacrifice. A good shepherd lays his life down for the sheep...

"Greater love has no man than this,
Than he lay down his life for his friends."
John 15:13

I planned to lay down My life for My friends *and* My enemies; even those who would stab Me in the back with betrayal, lay stripes upon Me — strip Me, beat Me and mock Me.

The character of a good shepherd who cares for His sheep is encapsulated in My Word... *"Shall I not drink the cup the Father has given Me?"*

"I am the good shepherd.
A good shepherd lays his life down for the sheep." John 10:11

I could see My Father in heaven as I pondered My weighty decision. I could see Him cheering Me on to ultimate victory. I could feel My Father's joy when He would greet Me at the end of My race, just as He will receive you with everlasting joy at the end of your race.

For the joy set before Me, I will endure the cross. What is My joy? *You* are My joy. Just as the Israelites smeared the lamb's blood on the posts and lintels of their doorways the night of the Passover in Egypt, for you, I am the blood of the Lamb spread over the doorway of your soul,

As the Angel of death swept through the land to smite the first born of every household, those in the dwellings covered in the blood of the lamb, were safe. The blood of the lamb symbolized the redemption of all who were in the house. In the same way, My blood is poured out for you —

so you can be saved from ultimate death. For now and forever, I am thinking of you.

I knew that tonight, before the orange sun rose over the Jerusalem horizon for the day of Preparation, my closest friends, would run and hide. Even Peter would deny Me three times. I knew, that even My beloved chosen children of Abraham, would gather in the morning and shout, "Crucify Him!"

My heart ached so deeply for my small band of eleven disciples, My precious students, My devoted followers. They were not much different from you. Some buyers, some sellers, some fishermen, some physicians, and even tax collectors, too. I recounted again the words that I had spoken to them at the Passover feast...

"A time is coming," I told them... *"when you will all fall away, for it is written, I will strike the shepherd, and the sheep will be scattered."*

Peter insisted quite adamantly, "Even if all fall away, I will not!"

"Yet," I said to Peter *"even tonight, before the rooster crows three times you will deny Me."*

"Never! I will *never* deny you! I will follow you to death!" Peter insisted.

I loved the persistent Peter. On him, I would build My church, not the outward church, but the inward church, My true church, the church of people's hearts. When two or three gather in My name, I am in the midst of them. The true church can take place in a building or in nature; it can have a name or not; but it is always a gathering of humble hearts who come together to worship Me, Jesus, their Messiah.

I had chosen the rock, Peter. I knew what he would do tonight, but I also knew what he would do only five weeks from now, on the Feast of *Shavuot*, when he will be filled with supernatural power, and proclaim My salvation on the steps of the temple. On this same day, also called Pentecost, he will proclaim the power and resurrection of the Messiah, Me, Jesus of Nazareth. He will prophesy in tongues, a heavenly language I will give to him. His prophetic language of tongues will be heard by his fellow Jewish people in twenty-seven different dialects.

This Feast of *Shavuot,* the Feast of the First Fruits, will be fulfilled, as the first fruits of the church are birthed that very day. But before this glorious day, Peter must endure his base emotions. He will face the human frailty of fear which will cause his faith to buckle. As I am condemned to be crucified, Peter will deny Me. It will be the most terrifying humiliation he has ever known; for a moment he will feel separated from his very Lord, His God. He will feel lost and naked, without the hope of redemption in his most raw display of human nature—just as you may feel when you are ashamed of Me, your God, your Lord, denying Me in your darkest hour...

If you are in darkness, call to Me and I will answer. I will illuminate your darkness for I am the Light of the World. Let Me be the light of *your* world. Trust Me in the darkness, for I am with you. When there is no light, take My hand. Let Me lead you, for I am your Savior, your Messiah, the One for whom you have been waiting. I lay down My life for you as the Good Shepherd of your soul, for I was thinking of you, as I am thinking of you now, just as I thought of Peter, of James, of John, My disciples...

These were not men with innate supernatural power. These were real Jewish men who had grown up in and around Jerusalem. They were hard working men with friends and families. They attended the temple, celebrated *Pesach* and *Purim* along with the other Feasts of Israel. They did not comprehend that their Rabbi Jesus, whom they had followed for the past three years, was certainly the Lamb of God to be slain, to take away the sins of the world.

They had walked closely with Me. All had left friends, families, homes and jobs to become my disciples. They had seen me raise the dead, heal the sick, make the lame to walk and the blind to see. Even Peter had witnessed the healing of his mother after she had laid with fever for many days. At the touch of My hands, she got up and began to cook for her son. My miracles poured out continually to those around Me. Many were never written down as they were too numerous to mention in a book.

My heart bled for Peter, for John, for James, who had sat so close to my feet. They had witnessed My power on earth. How could they understand that My power would be fulfilled in My death on the cross?

They had experienced the supernatural authority of their Messiah. The true Bread had come down from heaven to give life to the world. The true Bread had spent three years breaking bread with them, as well as blessing the miraculous five loaves and two fish which fed the 5,000.

I reminded them, *"To be of good courage, that I had overcome the world." John 16:33* But when the world turned against Me, the night of my trial, I looked defeated. They felt defeated as well.

Tonight, as they watched the events unfold in the Garden of Gethsemane, all seemed to be lost. Here were three years of their lives playing back before their eyes. Everything they had put their hope in for their future would be stripped, beaten, ridiculed, mocked and tried before *Caiaphas*, the high priest, who had advised the Jewish leaders that it would be good if one man died for the people.

My disciples cowered in terror and fled immediately as the detachment of soldiers along with their commander and the leaders of the temple officials arrested Me. One poor follower fled naked, having lost his robe. They grabbed him, but he escaped. I wanted him to escape. He was not the Lamb of God who would die this night. This pain and this glory would be Mine and Mine alone.

They bound My wrists. Not that they had to. I would have willingly gone with them. Peter and John now followed close behind Me as we walked first to the house of *Annais*, the father-in-law of *Caiaphas*. The soldier who wrapped my wrists pulled my arms so hard and the ropes so tight, that I might have dislocated my shoulder. He was used to a prisoner resisting arrest.

"Why is He not fighting?" The soldier thought to himself.

I was thinking of him... A soldier, who was simply doing his duty. How could he know he held the hands of God's own Son, the Anointed, the Christ? Even if he knew I was the chosen one of the Jewish people, it would not have mattered to him. He was not Jewish. He knew nothing of the temple, the laws, or the *Torah*.

He had to deal with the Jewish people on a daily basis since Rome was the supreme governmental power at the time. To him, the Passover only meant that the streets of Jerusalem would be overcrowded with foreigners who had come from all directions to celebrate the feast. There would also be holy men in their long robes reciting memorized prayers. The priests would be chanting blessings as the lambs were slaughtered. These rites and rituals meant nothing to this soldier. He was just doing his job. He did not know I was the Lamb of God to take away the sins of the world, as well as his sins, even those of his family.

He was a young man, only twenty-one, but had been married already three years. He had a family to feed and a demanding young wife who dreamed of going to Rome. He hoped one day he would be promoted to Captain or Centurion. I, to him, was simply an order to be carried out, a duty to be followed; yet there was something strange about the way he looked at Me. He may have wondered why he had to arrest such a mild-mannered man. He may have felt uneasy tethering Me and leading Me down the dusty road like a common criminal. He did not relish this responsibility of arresting a lowly Rabbi. He could not wait to release Me to the priests. To him, the long walk seemed to last an eternity.

How could he have known—the One whom he was holding in his taut grasp—held the keys to hell and death? How could he have known that before Abraham was, I Am? He may have thought I was a religious fraud. He may not have thought about Me at all, but all the while, I was thinking about him, just as I am thinking of you now...

One day, you might bind Me in your chains of judgments or take Me away to be tried in your court of calculated opinions—or perhaps the day comes when what other people think of Me causes you to act in a way you would not ordinarily act, because, like this soldier— you are just doing your job. Perhaps you never question their opinions. Perhaps you do question them but do not want to make any waves or cause any problems. By questioning, you might lose your position in the government, society, or your position in the Roman Legion for that matter.

I wondered if this soldier *knew* Me, would he release Me?

Perhaps, but that would not happen now. No, tonight he would carry out his duty, for it is My destiny to be brought before the Sanhedrin. It is for this reason I must die. For you, for this soldier—for ignorance, for defiance, for compliance... I must die, for I was thinking of you, just as I am thinking of you now...

I love you. You can find forgiveness. Don't turn away. Look to Me, the Lamb of God. I came for My own, the lost sheep of Israel, but they did not receive Me. As many as receive Me, I give the right to be sons and daughters of God, just as this soldier could become My son if he humbled himself before Me.

"Behold the Lamb of God who takes away the sins of the World!" John the Baptist had proclaimed when he baptized Me. At that moment, a dove descended from heaven and My Father's voice spoke, also from heaven...

"This is My son, I am very pleased with Him."

Matthew 3:17

The Light shone in the darkness, but the darkness did not comprehend the light. The light reveals men's and women's hearts, whether they are good or evil.

"Yahuweh dwells with those who are of a contrite and humble spirit."
Isaiah 57:15

Even though the priests of the *Torah* had studied about Me in Isaiah, Zechariah, and the Psalms... they did not recognize Me.

Some of the Jewish leaders had come to Me in secret and in the night. Joseph of Arimethia, who would donate his tomb to me, was one of them. How curious these teachers were to learn more about Me. How open they were to the truth. How pure their hearts were as they composed their questions...

"How can one be born again? How can a man re-enter his mother's womb?" Nicodemus asked. He was one of the priests who humbly addressed Me as a teacher, Rabbi. "Rabbi, we know that You are a teacher come from God; for no one can do these signs that You do unless God is with him."

Knowing that I had come from God, he was indeed on the edge of the most crucial truth in the universe.

I answered...

"To enter the kingdom of God, one must be born of the Spirit."

Nicodemus said to Me, "How can a man be born when he is old? Can he enter a second time into his mother's womb and be born?"

I answered...

"Most assuredly, I say to you, unless one is born of water
And the Spirit, he cannot enter the kingdom of God.
That which is born of the flesh is flesh, and that which is born of the Spirit
is spirit.
Do not marvel that I said to you, 'You must be born again.'
The wind blows where it wishes, and you hear the sound of it,
But cannot tell where it comes from and where it goes.
So is everyone who is born of the Spirit."
John 3:5

To be born of the flesh is to be born into sin. The world is fallen and perverse, held captive to the sin of Adam. To be born of the Spirit is to have one's eyes open—to understand the mystery of the Messiah.

Here I was, the anointed One, Emanuel, the Mighty God, the Prince of Peace, the Lion of the tribe of Judah, the One to whom the scepter of *Shiloh* was passed; but in the Jewish leader's jots and tittles and the dotting of the i's; lost in the ordinances and the extensive rabbinical laws where they exacted their labors as they argued each point—they could not recognize the very Truth they had been looking for. The Son of God stood before them—the grace of *Adonai* gloried in their midst.

In their zeal, they had searched the scriptures but they did not come to Me. How could they not *know* Me? I loved each one! How I hoped they would recognize Me, but alas, a hard heart has blind eyes.

"Oh, Jerusalem, Jerusalem, how you stone those who are sent to you.

After tonight, your temple will be left to you desolate.

How I longed to gather you as a hen gathers her chicks."

Matthew 23:37

These words I will speak as I stagger up the hill to Golgotha in the morning, bloody, beaten and worn. Why didn't they see the compassion in My eyes? Couldn't they tell I was not putting up a fight? What were they so afraid of?

Often those who are most afraid are the ones who accuse and condemn others. So, for these priests, or for anyone who would ever condemn an innocent man to die, I must die in their place, in order to make a way of salvation, for anyone who calls upon My name.

If it is you… if you have stood in the judgment seat for someone in your own life, if you have condemned someone to die, or if you are trapped under the weight of your own law to the point you cannot see your Messiah, then it is for you I must die. When you have exacted your labors until your heart is stone cold—you need to know you are still loved and can be forgiven, if you call upon Me—you can find forgiveness in Me.

It was for My misguided religious rulers I had to die and for the soldiers herding me to my execution—and for you.

For after all, I was thinking of you, as I am thinking of you now…

Setting...
Palace of Caiaphas

Luke 22:66-71; Luke 23:1-24

As I walked, bound and chained, into the inner court of the temple to stand before the Council of the Sanhedrin, I recounted these words written by the prophet Isaiah,

"All day I have stretched out My hands to a stubborn people,
Who walk in the way which is not good, following their own thoughts."

Isaiah 65:2

It comforted Me to know that Isaiah was inspired years before to write these prophetic words. I was assured that My prophet Isaiah wrote his book and spoke to the people according to the inspiration of the *R'uach H'kodesh,* The Holy Spirit, even though he saw himself as "a man with unclean lips."

When he had his prophetic calling, Isaiah wrote...

"...I saw the Lord sitting on a throne, high and lifted up, and the train of His robe filled the temple.

Above it stood seraphim; each one had six wings...

And one cried to another and said: 'Holy, holy, holy is the Lord of hosts; The whole earth is full of His glory!' And the posts of the door were shaken by the voice of him who cried out, and the house was filled with smoke.

So I said: 'Woe is me, for I am undone!
Because I am a man of unclean lips,
And I dwell in the midst of a people of unclean lips;
For my eyes have seen the King, The Lord of hosts.'

Isaiah 6:5

One day, My people of Israel will look on Me, Jesus—the One whom they will pierce tomorrow on their passover. One day, at the end of the age, after the great tribulation, when I descend in the clouds, with the sound of a great trumpet and gather My saints from the four winds of the earth—I will stand on the Mount of Olives once again—not as a humble Messiah, but as a reigning King.

At that time, all people of the earth shall see Me.

"That at the name of Jesus every knee should bow, of those in heaven,
And of those on earth, and of those under the earth, and that every tongue
should confess that Jesus Christ is Lord, to the glory of God the Father."

Philippians 2:10-11

One day when the future nation of Israel is a generation old, there will be signs and wonders throughout the earth, the moon will turn to blood, the sun with be darkened. One day when you see the Revelation 12 sign align in the stars—of the virgin, clothed with the sun, with the moon at her feet, wearing a crown of twelve stars on her head, look up! Your redemption is near. *

"When these things begin to happen, stand up and lift up your heads,
Because your redemption is drawing near."

Luke 21:28

One day… One day… But that day was not today.

For nearly two thousand years after My death and resurrection, most of My people of Israel will be trapped in darkness. A thick veil will lie over their hearts whenever the law of Moses is read as they are scattered to the ends of the earth. At that same time, Jerusalem will be trodden down as the Gentile church age flourishes, until one day, after a seven-day war,** Israel will inhabit Jerusalem again. At this time the Gentile Church Age will be fulfilled, and the veil will begin to be lifted from the eyes of My Jewish people. *Luke 21:24*

The One who stood before them now was their righteous Messiah. I had come to fulfill the law. I was not the prisoner here. The prisoners who stood before Me were the Pharisees and Sadducees—prisoners to their own rules and regulations. I had come to set them free.

It was for these false leaders I had to die, but it is also for you, when you are trapped under the weight of your own law, religion or set of rules. Open your eyes. Look at Me. I will die so that *you* can enter in—to the Holy of Holies—the inner room of the temple, where the glory of God is.

The Holy of Holies in Jerusalem, or *Kodesh haKodashim,* of the temple, also called the "Inner House" was thirty feet in length, breadth, and height. It exhibited floors and wainscot of cedar of Lebanon, and its walls and floor were overlaid with gold. It contained two cherubim of olive-wood, each fifteen feet high and each having outspread wings of fifteen feet span, so that, since they stood side by side, the wings touched the wall on either side and met in the center of the room. *I Kings 6*

There was a two-leaved door between it and the Holy Place overlaid with gold; also a veil of blue, purple, and crimson and fine linen. It had no windows and was considered the dwelling-place of the "name" of God. The Holy of Holies housed the Ark of the Covenant; containing the original tablets of the Ten Commandments.

When the priests emerged from the Holy place after placing the Ark there, the Temple was filled with a cloud, "For the glory of the Lord had filled the house of the Lord." *2 Chronicles 3-5; I Kings 6-8*

You will no longer need a high priest to enter in to the Holy of Holies, you will have a Savior. For when I die, the veil—the curtain of the temple which separates the Holy of Holies from the common man will be torn—from top to bottom. Torn completely, replaced by My blood, so there will be nothing but the Messiah. I am the Holy of Holies. *Matthew 27:51; Mark 15:38*

I have come to take away the *veil* from your eyes.
"Where the Spirit of the Lord and where the Spirit of the Lord is,
There is liberty."
II Corinthians 3:17

God has given no one else authority in this earth and in heaven to give My followers access to Him. For it is written,
"God, Elohim, who at various times and in diverse manners spoke in the
past to the fathers by the prophets
has in these last days spoken unto us by his Son,
Whom He has appointed, chosen to be heir of all things,
By whom also He made the world.
Who being the brightness of His glory, and the express image of His person
And upholding all things by the words of His power,
When he had by Himself cleansed, purged, made atonement for our sins,
Sat down on the right hand of the Majesty on high.
For the Son, being made so much better than the angels has by
inheritance obtained a more excellent name than they
For unto which of the angels has He said,
'You are My Son, this day I have created you and given you birth,
And again. I will be to him a Father, and He shall be to me a Son?'
And to whom has Adonai said,

'Let all the angels of God worship Him?' This He only said to the Son.
Yahuweh says, 'Thy throne, Oh God, is forever and ever, the authority,
The scepter of righteousness is the scepter of thy kingdom.
Because You have loved righteousness, and have hated iniquity,
Therefore, God, even God has anointed you, the anointed One,
The Messiah, the Savior of the whole world.'"
Hebrews 1:1-13

What kind of God would have authority without compassion? I am the compassion of God. Jesus is the face of God, the tangible God, sacrificing Himself for your sins. I, Jesus, the fulfillment of the 328 prophesies of the Messiah in the *Tanakh,* am the Messiah, the door one must open to find intimate fellowship with the Creator of the universe.

I stood silently before the teachers of the *Torah*—meditating on these words in My heart. Meanwhile, the leaders of the council grew uneasy. My silence unnerved them...

Their blood was boiling in their veins, as they hurled accusations at Me, each one landing like a black stone thrown into a field, a field, pure white with newly fallen snow. In the ancient courts of justice in Israel, the accused were condemned with black stones and those found innocent were acquitted with white stones. Even before the black stone was thrown down, their black stoney hearts pummeled Me with their accusations, "Tell us if you are the Messiah!"

I answered...

"If I tell you, you will not believe Me,
But from now on the Son of Man will be seated at the right hand of God."
Romans 8:34

The Pharisees and Sadducees jeered louder, "Are you the Son of God?"

I replied...

"You are right in saying I am..."

The Word cut the air with a double-edged sword—right through to the intentions of their hearts. The Word that discerns the intentions of their hearts. The Word that divides between soul and spirit.

Their hearts were being revealed. The innermost purposes and desires were being stripped naked and the secret sins of their hearts were being laid bare. The scene was much like the day they had caught the woman in adultery. They brought her to Me and demanded the punishment of death by stoning as it is written in the *Torah*.

In order to expose the hypocrisy of their condemnation, I began to write their sins in the sand. As I wrote, I said…

"Let he who is among you without sin cast the first stone…"

John 8:7

The crowd backed away as the sins written in the sand revealed their most hidden thoughts and actions. They murmured among themselves. "Who is He? One who spoke with such authority?"

I was thinking of the woman caught in adultery, as I was thinking of you — as I am thinking of you now, when you may catch the person you love being unfaithful to you or when you might lie in wait to call out the sins of your neighbor or a person sitting next to you in your church or synagogue.

Just like these religious leaders. I am not lying in wait to condemn you. I am dying to save you from Judgment. Yes, the punishment for adultery as written in the *Torah* is death, but you have a Messiah who is standing in the way of the stones, just I was taking false accusations being hurled at Me tonight.

I will take the punishment for you, as I complete the walk to the cross, to be crucified, to die for the sins that you, your loved one or your neighbor may commit; so that when you or they are dragged into a public square and the crowd gathers around to stone you or them, with their rules and law, I am thinking of you. I am being punished for you. My soul is poured out to death for you, so that when — for your sins, you deserve to die, I will have paid the price for you. I am your ransom.

When you cry out for mercy, your Savior, the Lamb of God, is the Mercy seat. My Father forgives you in My name, for I am the righteous Messiah who atones for the sin of the world. I am *Yeshua*, which means *Yahuweh* saves, the only name given for which men and women can be saved.

As I watched the Pharisees and Sadducees rant and rave, I was remembering the day I stood up in the temple, on the Feast of *Sukkot*, the Feast of Tabernacles, the first day of My ministry, when I began to quote from Isaiah 61, "the Spirit of the Lord is upon Me, because He has anointed Me to preach the gospel to the poor: He has sent Me to heal the broken-hearted, to proclaim liberty to the captive, and recovery of sight to

45

the blind, to set at liberty those who are oppressed, to proclaim the acceptable year of the Lord."

After I spoke these words, I closed the *Torah*, gave it back to the steward and sat down.

All the eyes of the synagogue were fixed on Me, as I proclaimed...

"Today this scripture is fulfilled in your ears."

A chaotic assembly conferred with one another, "Isn't this Joseph's son? How is it He speaks with the authority of God?" *Luke 4:18-22*

This they spoke before they threw Me out of the Synagogue.

Tonight, much like that day, but with escalated hostility and greater hatred and jealousy, these 'keepers of the *Torah*' continued to hurl stones across the room. Out of the abundance of the heart, the mouth speaks, and they were each proving the constitution of their own heart, as they hurled black stones, each one in my direction. "Guilty! Guilty! Guilty!"

An unclean soot consisting of the stains of their own guilty conscience left a residue on their hands. After accusing God's own Son this night, they would wash their hands many times but never will their hands feel clean again.

I grieved deeply on account of the ugliness of their hearts. They were the ones whom I had called out to be separate, to walk closely with Me. I wanted to say, "Come to Me. Find forgiveness."

"Though you forget Me, I will not forget you.

I have inscribed you on the palms of My hands." Isaiah 49:16

As they brought the prison bars down upon Me, insisting I was guilty, they were really bringing Judgment on themselves.

"Where will your blood sacrifice be, you teachers of the law, after the temple is destroyed?" I wanted to shout. "Where is your sacrifice? How will you justify yourselves without the perfect lamb of God to atone for your sins? How are your good works going to give you entrance into the Holy of Holies? Rabbinical laws will not be enough to give you entrance into the kingdom of heaven."

"TELL US! Are You the Messiah, the Son of God?" They continued to buffet Me. But I knew as they questioned, they did not want an answer.

"Yes, it is as you say, I Am HE." I said to them, as I say to you.

"In the future you will see the Son of man sitting at the right band of the The Almighty, coming on the clouds of heaven." Matthew 24:30

46

Then the High Priest tore his clothes and shouted, "He has spoken blasphemy! Why do we need any more witnesses? Look, now you have heard this blasphemy. What do you think?"

"HE IS WORTHY OF DEATH!" They all shouted.

Then they spat in My face and struck Me. The soldiers began to pound my face with their fists, shouting, "Prophesy! Prophesy who hit you!"

Now was the hour for darkness to reign...

As they pummeled My visage, unblemished and calm, I remained silent. I didn't say a word, for I was thinking of you, as I am thinking of you now...

As they spat in My face, I thought of Isaiah's prophecy concerning Me.

"He was despised, rejected of men. We esteemed Him not.
Surely He took up our infirmities and carried our sorrows.
He was silent. He opened not His mouth." Isaiah 53

I said to the Pharisees and Sadducees,

"Every day I was with you in the Temple, but you did not lay a hand on Me."

Now I kept silent and would be silent to the end. I opened not My mouth. A Lamb led to the slaughter for you, for them, for all who have sinned and fallen short of the glory of God. There was not any other way,. I am the Way. For I was thinking of you, as I am thinking of you now...

When you have hit a dead end in your road of good works, when you have laid one law upon another, stretching out a ladder of rules, rung by rung, making a ladder up to heaven only to find out it is too short to reach the Holy dwelling place of God—look to the Lamb of *Yahuweh*. My blood covers the sins of the whole world. Look to the Messiah who endured the rejection of men, humbled Himself unto death and is now seated at the right hand of the Father in heaven—a heavenly door opened to you made possible by My blood, the blood of Jesus, the Righteous Messiah of Israel. A door for anyone who calls on His name.

"I am the door of the sheep, the Good Shepherd."

Call on My name now. I love you... for after all, I was thinking of you as I am thinking of you now....

*Revelation 12:1 Sign happened in the heavens at The Feast of Trumpets
September 22-23, 2017 depending on where you viewed it 2017
**Seven Day War 1967

Setting...
Jesus being led from the Court of the Sanhedrin to stand before Pontius Pilate

Luke 22:63-65

The priests of the temple of Jerusalem, chosen from the tribes of Aaron and Levi, who were to minister before Me, burn incense to Me, sacrifice to Me—came together tonight with one goal in mind—to eradicate Me, their Messiah, from their religious domain and from the face of the earth. They lead the people in the *Eluhenu,* yet their *Adonai* in the flesh stood before them and they did not recognize Me.

I was still bound and bleeding profusely from the beating I had just received, as they led Me, to be accused before Pontuis Pilate, the Governor of Rome. The soldiers had spit in My face, pounded Me with their fists, hit me in the head, then blind-folded Me, shouting, "Prophesy! Prophesy! Who is it who hit you? Tell us, if you are the Messiah!"

Many other insults were hurled at Me. Insults which were intended to injure Me as much as the physical blows, but I spoke not a word. I remained silent. I did not retaliate in anger, for I was thinking of them—as I was thinking of you, as I am thinking of you now...

When you are not happy with the way I am running things, when you have come to insult Me, your Savior, your Lord—when you bind Me in your opinions and blindfold Me, hoping I cannot see—while you smite Me in the face with your doubts, fears, and criticisms. When you find momentary safety, surrounded by a small group of persons, also insulting Me, and even if you do not initiate the hitting, you find your hand raised in the fever of their fervor to possibly even punch My face, I am in the midst —thinking of you.

If you insult Me, use My name in vain, or if you raise your hand to strike a child, or assert control over a person physically weaker, than you— as you strike, perhaps out of ignorance or perhaps out of fear, you are the one who is blindfolded, not Me. You are the one who is weak, not them.

"Whatever has been done in secret will be brought out into the light."

Luke 8:17

I am here to say, that what you have done to these little ones, you have done unto Me. And it is for you, on the day when you realize what you have done and you are truly sorry—when your hands are stained with innocent blood and there is no way to undo the past—it is for this moment I came to die. It is for you I keep silent as I walk this lonely path to the execution that awaits Me at *Golgatha*. For when the sentence of death awaits you; I, the Lamb of God, the Messiah, the Savior of the whole world will have accepted that sentence of death for you.

All men and women are dead men walking, sentence set, but even now, I am walking in your shoes—I love you. In Me there is no death. I am taking away death and will swallow it up in victory. I was thinking of you, as I am thinking of you now.

Drops of blood spilled onto the arms of my assailants. These were not like the drops of blood spilling down my cheeks—those of self-sacrifice in the garden. No, these were drops of blood springing forth from an innocent man, thrashed beyond recognition. As My blood ran onto their arms and hands, they failed to realize that just one drop of My blood shed for each of them was enough to atone for their blood-stained hands. One drop of My blood is enough to atone for the blood on your hands—your sins—now and forever, atoned, covered, paid for.

Forgiven with one drop of My blood poured out for you, even for the sins of these men, leading the Messiah, the Savior of the whole world to the cross—even your sins as you lead Me to your own cross, nail Me with your defiance and crucify Me with your silence. The drops of My blood running down My cheeks from the blows of your hands, as you have hit Me with your demands, is spilling on your hands, as you walk your sentence, all the while, sentencing Me.

As I am condemned in a crowd as a fraud, and you remain quiet—I am still walking silently to the cross—all the while, proclaiming you free. I will become your advocate, when I sit down at the right hand of the Father.

I will walk alone to the death seat today for your atonement, so that, as you walk alone one day, to the judgment seat of God—you can stop, before you get there. Lift up your eyes. Look at Me. You can find forgiveness with just one breath uttered to Me in humility. Lift the blindfold you have put on My eyes. Lift the blindfold and you will see Me, looking at you with eyes of love.

I kept silent. I did not defend Myself as the soldiers struck Me, for in My silence, I was defending them. I was praying silently...

"Father, 'Forgive them, for they don't know what they are doing.'"

Luke 23:34

I had to die for them for they did not know what they were doing, just as you so often will not know what you are doing.

The original sin seemed like the right thing to do, when Adam and Eve were tempted to eat of the *one* tree God had said NOT to eat of. They questioned God's command to eat of any tree, "Except the tree of the knowledge of good and evil...of this you shall *not* eat...on the day that you eat of it, you will surely die." *Genesis 2:17*

A day is as a thousand years and a thousand years as a day to the Lord. Peter 3:8

Adam and Eve had reasoned between themselves. "Why would God not want us to know good from evil? Why would He not want us to eat of *every* tree in the Garden?"

Their failure was one of obedience and trust. They failed to simply obey, which is a lack of trust. If they trusted their Creator, acknowledging that He knew what was best for them—they would not haven eaten of the forbidden fruit.

They also lacked the fear of the Lord. It is written, "The fear of the Lord is the beginning of knowledge." *Proverbs 1:7* Adam and Eve at that moment did not trust their God, nor did they fear Him; so, instead of obeying the Lord their God when they were lied to, they forsook the tree of life, which possesses the very root of true knowledge and bears the fruit of wisdom, and succumbed to the serpent's lies instead, "You shall be like god."

Also, their pride led them to eat of the tree. Even though Adam and Eve were already made in Our image, the image of *Elohim*, they wanted more. If they had been humble, like children, they would have been content with the beautiful, perfect environment of the Garden. Instead, they wanted to be like god which really means, being the same as God, in the same hierarchy; thus, worshipped as God, just as Lucifer wanted to be worshipped as God, which caused him to be cast down from heaven along with one-third of the angels, who are now demons roaming the earth.

51

I knew they would sin in the garden, and when found naked, put a fig leaf over their private parts, just as I know you might sin one day when you turn from Me, forsake the tree of life, and instead, eat the fruit from the tree of good and evil. It will taste so good at first, after you are tempted with that first delicious bite... of death. You may not have thought one bite would lead you to death, but when you decided to partake of a lie, the digestion of a one lie after another, causes you to become intoxicated with lies.

God had said to Adam and Eve, "If you eat of this tree...on the day that you eat of it, you will surely die." *Genesis 2:17* And they did die that day...

"A day is as a thousand years and a thousand years as a day to the Lord."
Peter 3:8

Neither Adam nor Eve, nor any other human being has lived on earth to be 1,000 years old. And, of course, faced an ultimate death, separation from God.

When you find yourself naked, exposed and alone, separated from Truth, you might place a fig leaf over your private thoughts, to hide from Me, rather than to admit you may have been wrong, and that, perhaps— God is right after all. You have just eaten the forbidden fruit along with Adam and Eve,

"For just as the serpent beguiled Eve and Adam through his subtle lies...
so you might be corrupted from the simplicity that is found in
Jesus the Messiah." 2 Corinthians 11:13

It is written,

"Thou shalt not have any other gods before Me." Exodus 20:3

Yet, so often you place yourself before Me as your own god. You decide for yourself what is right and wrong, rather than simply obey My commandments. You might even put your religion or rules before Me, deciding your traditions are more important then Me.

I am in your midst, the One, True and living God, yet you may desire to worship an old set of rules, rather than to worship the I Am that I Am—and have fellowship with Me, as Adam and Eve did at first, in the Garden —and really *know* Me.

Here I was on the path to Pilate, their Messiah, the *Adonai* of Israel, the God of Gods, the One who is God, stumbling down a dusty path, —bleeding for them. But their pride had blinded them. They had exalted their own revelation. Oh, how they searched the *Torah*, yet it is the *Torah* which speaks of Me. I stood before them, as I stand before them now, and they do not come to Me that they might *know* Me, their own Messiah. Some do, but many do not.

"Search the scriptures; for in them you think ye have eternal life:
and they are they which testify of Me and you will not come to Me
That you might have eternal life."

John 5:39-40

I spoke to the Rabbis in the temple...

"Your father Abraham rejoiced to see my day:
When he saw it, he was glad."

They replied, "You are not even fifty years old. Have you seen Abraham?" I answered to them...

"Truly I say this to you...Before Abraham was, I am." John 8:54-58

The religious leaders had picked up stones to throw at Me, just as you sometimes pick up your stones to throw at Me. Perhaps the stones they threw originated in their stoney hearts. Perhaps you have a heap of rubble ready to throw at Me when things don't go your way—when the very fact that there is one God who interrupts your selfish motives or your plans that might not be My will, but yours.

Sometimes a lie is easier to swallow than the truth, just like the bite Adam and Eve took in the Garden. A lie goes down easily. It might not get caught in your throat, but it will not produce the righteous fruit God desires.

The fruit of the lie begins to rot. Somehow, in the pit of the stomach of your soul, the lies you have eaten begin to mold, then poison emanates from the lies and seeps into the stream of your psyche which then permeates your entire system of beliefs; affecting your emotions and your mind—a poison which is pumped through your heart and eventually comes out of your mouth—causing you to say and do things you might not ordinarily want to do.

"A good man out of the good treasure of his heart brings forth good;
And an evil man out of the evil treasure of his heart brings forth evil.
For out of the abundance of the heart his mouth speaks."

Luke 6:45

As you have chosen to eat the lie of the tree of knowledge of good and evil with the desire to be like a god, you are now on the throne of your own life, ruling your own universe from your self-centered kingdom. You lust for more knowledge yet forget the Maker and Creator of your soul. Then you become lost in a labyrinth of these lies and find yourself forever circling back to the entrance of the maze you got yourself into—the place or time where you ate the forbidden fruit, just like Adam and Eve.

You are now cast out into the wilderness of endless knowledge, yet void of peace, because you are now under a curse, just as Adam and Eve fell under the curse when they were cast out of the Garden. There is no redemption after eating from the forbidden tree other than to eat of the tree of life—except now the entrance to the Garden of Eden, where the tree of life stands, is a forbidden paradise guarded by two huge cherubim angels with swords.

In the beginning, God knew Adam and Eve would sin. He also knew you would sin, thus he wrote the plan of redemption into the story. The seed of the woman would rise up to crush the serpent and his lies and...

Here I am, the tree of life, standing before you. *I am He.*

Jeremiah prophesied. "The days are coming, says the Lord, when I will make a new covenant with the house of Israel, with the house of Judah, not according to the covenant that I made with their fathers in the day that I took them by the hand to bring them out of the land of Egypt. This will be the covenant that I will make with the house of Israel. I will put my law in their inward parts and write in their hearts. I will be their God, and they will be My people." *Jeremiah 31:31*

At the last supper I celebrated with My Disciples, I said to them,
"Take this bread. This is my body which is given for you. Also, drink this cup. This is the new covenant in My blood which is shed for you."
Matthew 26:26
"I am the living bread which came out of heaven. If any one eats of this bread, he shall live forever. The bread is My body which I give for the life of the world. Except that you eat of the body of the Son of man, The Messiah Jesus, and drink His blood, you have no life in you."
John 6:51
"Whoever eats of my flesh and drinks My blood has eternal life And I will raise him or her up on the last day."
John 6:54

Blood symbolizes life which belongs to God. My blood poured out for you is the eternal life nectar of the fruit of the tree of life, the atonement for your sins. I said to My people Israel—

"If you do not believe that I am He, you will die in your sins."
John 8:24

There is no other way. This is the way. The way of redemption. The way back to the Garden—not the Garden of Eden, but to the throne of Heaven and eternal life—the Eternal Garden.

"For God so loved the world: He gave his one and only Son
That everyone who believes in him should not perish but have eternal life.
For God did not send his Son into the world to condemn the world,
But that the world should be saved through him.
The one who believes in Him is not condemned.
The one who does not believe has been condemned already, because he has
not believed in the name of the One and only Son of God."
John 3:16-18

As I pressed on in the wee hours of the morning just before dawn —I was *with* the soldiers, but I was not *of* them. I was *with* the leaders of the temple, but not *of* them— each of their steps was coated in the blood of guilt as they led their Messiah, the Chosen One of *Adonai*, to be sentenced before Pilate. I could have been paving their path to paradise with each drop of blood that fell into each of their footprints—if they had chosen Me. If they would have humbled themselves before Me, each and every step of their pride and ignorance could have been atoned for—forgiven.

I paved this path of redemption, in sorrow, in suffering—for I was thinking of you, as I am thinking of you now...

For this reason I took each painful step, felt each drop of blood seep from my broken body, without saying a word.

Setting...
Jesus en route from the court of the Sanhedrin to be accused before Pilate.

Luke 22: 31-43;54-62

My captors and I passed by a group of people gathered outside the temple. I saw Peter in the distance—with his back turned to Me. He had valiantly promised to protect me. He had bravely followed Me to the courtyard. But when the Roman guards slammed the door to the inner court in Peter's face, he sheepishly backed down. He had lingered in the shadows for a little while—as close as he possibly could be to Me. A cluster of commons folks were warming their hands by a fire.

Peter slowly moved to join them, thinking he could be incognito. Instead of warming his hands, his hands were perspiring. He was wringing them, almost too harshly. His heart beat rapidly. He tried to stop wringing his hands. "The group will notice," he thought to himself.

I knew Peter would *not* be with Me anymore at this point, yet what he did not know—is that I was *with* him. As his fellow Jewish colleagues eyed him suspiciously, I was thinking of him.

They stared at him, eyes reflecting the flames of the fire. Peter cast his eyes to the ground. The fire seemed much hotter than any previous fire he could ever remember. The flames seemed to leap off the logs and sear into his heart. He concentrated on the wildly dancing flames, blue, orange, red. He didn't dare look up. Even though he had not looked up, he felt that everyone was glaring at him.

He felt the eyes of those near him watch his every move. He felt he was being surveyed from every side. He felt that if the eyes of those near him would shut or turn away, that the eyes of the universe would keep staring—eyes of stars, of moon, of sun, even all of the heavenly host—eyes which would penetrate his fearful heart with their relentless stare. "Those eyes," his mind raced, "those eyes..." he grabbed his head.

"Why are you staring at ME?" he wanted to scream, "Stop it!"

He silently shouted within himself over and over. "Why is everyone looking at me? Stop looking at me!"

His heart, beating loudly, did not seem like an organ of his body anymore, but a vast echoing chamber of eternal weights and balances. Decisions and destinies to be determined—with the eyes watching him as the jury and the intentions of his heart as the judge, "He is guilty!" They silently screamed.

"I must not forsake Him." Peter's mind tried reign in his thoughts to focus on the *why* and *what* of the moment. "I must focus on Him, my Messiah, my Lord."

The past three years in which he had followed Me, flashed back before him. He was with Me—when I said to Lazarus, who had lain dead in his grave already four days...

"Lazarus...Come forth!" John 11:43

Peter could hardly believe his eyes as Lazarus appeared at the entrance of the tomb. Peter had eagerly stepped forward to help unwrap the grave clothes of a man who was dead and now lived.

He had seen Me raise the widow's son. Heal the lepers. Make the lame man get up, carry his bed and walk. He had seen Me walk on water. He had even come to meet Me, stepping out onto the water with great faith for a brief moment. Right before he began to sink, he had recognized Me as the Son of God when he proclaimed, "Surely, You are the Messiah, the Son of God." *Mathew 16:16*

He recounted My words I had spoken to him earlier this evening...
"Simon, Simon, (for that was his name before he became Peter, the rock),
Simon, behold, satan has desired to have you, that he may sift you
As wheat, but I have prayed for you, that your faith will not fail.
When you are converted, strengthen your brethren."

"Lord, I am ready to go with you, both into prison and to death!" He remembered his response and was surprised at Mine...
"I tell you, Peter, the rooster will not crow this day before you
have denied Me, not once, but three times."
Luke 22:31-34

Peter replayed every word in his head, "I cannot forsake him. I will not forsake him." Peter was determined, but as the inquisition of eyes circled around him, getting closer and closer, he began to burn on a stake of fear, failure and doubt.

"I know *He* would never forsake me." He reassured himself.

Peter leapt to his feet. "I must not forsake him!" He yelled so loudly in his mind, he was sure that everyone had heard him. He glanced nervously around. No. No one was looking at him. Except, maybe her or maybe him...?

The fire seemed to snarl as if a thousand demons were mocking him with lashing tongues, "You fool! You followed a failure! And now, you, too, will die with him! What were you thinking? Why did you leave everything to go with this man? You had a thriving business. You thought you were going to do something important to save Israel? Ha! You are nothing but a scared fisherman."

He was Peter, one of Jesus' closest disciples. Now his Lord, his Messiah, was inside the inner court of the Sanhedrin being accused of blasphemy. Peter, outside the court, was enduring his own trial. In the court of satan, Lucifer sifted, sifted, sifted Peter, as one sifts wheat on a threshing floor...

The threshing floor was the place where sheaves of grain were crushed under the feet of oxen. The partly threshed grain was continually being turned over with a fork. The stalks became broken into short pieces and the husks of grain separated from the stalk. The mixture of chaff and grain was then thrown into the wind with a winnowing fork. The chaff blew away and the good grain was collected in a pile. The stalks were often burned. The entire process of threshing is about refining the edible wheat from the unusable parts of the grain. The refinement that comes from sifting makes the grain usable and creates seed for producing a future harvest—a harvest producing one hundred times more crop. Without the sifting, the good wheat is essentially useless.

Peter would one day become a usable seed on which I could plant My church on the day of the Feast of *Shavuot*. Alas, tonight he was on the threshing floor, enduring the most excoriating testing of his life being accused by the enemy of his soul....

I told Peter I had prayed for him—that his faith would not fail. Also, I was praying for him, as I am praying for you, for after all— I was thinking of him, as I am thinking of you now... as you wrestle with the voices that lie to your soul during your own time of testing, when shouts of cynicism war against the truth and attack the most profound beliefs in your heart.

When satan sifts you on the threshing floor of faith, stomping on you with questions and doubts of My Lordship and eternal life — the enemy of your soul stares at you with a million eyes of strangers piercing into the stark naked core of your being shouting — "What do you believe?!"

I have prayed for you, just as I prayed for Peter. I have prayed that your faith would not fail.

"Surely He *is* the Messiah." Peter kept trying to keep his thoughts on course as He saw me bound in chains. "Truly He is the Son of God, the Son of David, the Righteous Messiah who had come to deliver His people Israel. Why, then, is he being sentenced?"

"Yes," Peter concentrated with all of his might on the truth that he knew, as he paced back and forth, back and forth, his mind now in a wrestling match — lies lapping against truth in a ring of fire.

"Truth! He is surely the Messiah," his heart said. "Lies! How could that be true? He was just a carpenter from Nazareth."

His brain pulsated in anguish — with lies, lies — just as lies pound your brain, during your time of sifting, as you lay bare on the sifting floor. Like massive waves pummeling you, set after set, when you have swam past the breakwater, you are losing strength, and you cannot take one more wave — this is the moment of your own truth, as this riptide of lies attempts to drown you in fear, the shore of faith seems distant, out of reach, especially when all you have gained, you think may be lost.

Even though Peter attempted to steer the conversation with himself straight through the tumultuous waters of deceit to stay focused on the truth, he began to capsize — his attempts were ruthlessly tossed, feeling somewhat like steering a boat into the eye of a perfect storm.

As the hurricane-like winds of doubts, half-truths, empty words and accusations sent waves to hit his small craft, Peter felt the full wrath from the wicked blows of the sifting. Doubts like sharks bearing teeth — that thrash truth in the jaws of hell, relentlessly, until the victim wonders if he has ever known any God at all.

"I am the Way, the Truth, the Life."

Peter had heard Me say...

"No one comes to the Father, but by Me."

John 14:6

"I and the Father are One"
John 10:30

These were radical statements, yet Peter's eyes were opened. He could see. He had been with Me at the Mount of Transfiguration when Moses and Elijah appeared. Peter had tried to speak, but a bright cloud overshadowed them and a voice spoke out of the cloud.

"This is my beloved Son, whom I love.
I am very pleased with him. Listen to Him."
Matthew 17:5

When Peter and the other disciples heard the voice, they were terrified and fell on their faces, until I touched them and said...

"Do not be afraid."

Oh, how Peter wished I could touch him now—how he wished that the heavens would open up and the voice of God would speak into this dismal moment and say, "Ha ha, the seemingly cruel joke is over. Your Savior is not being condemned to die. It'll all be over in the morning and He will be back together with you."

But alas, this is My hour of darkness. Faith is tested in darkness. This was also the hour of Peter's darkness. Peter was being sifted like wheat, dividing the grain from the chaff— winnowing the windows of his soul, his beliefs, and his secret heart.

And yet the fear of being accused of being a follower of Me, was a different fear than the fear he felt, when the voice spoke out of heaven. He remembered this voice—the voice of many waters—a voice that had brought him to his knees. Yes, he was afraid of this voice, but it was also strong and soothing, calm, and in control.

The voices of fear inside his head, however, were vastly different. They brought confusion, condemnation, and darkness.

All the while I was thinking of him, as the voice of a servant girl seated near him by the fire who had been examining him closely, broke the screaming silence of his inner turmoil, "This man was with Jesus!"

"Woman, I don't know him!" Peter lashed back at her before he even had time to think.

"You *are* one of them!" a man next to him called out.

"Man, I am not!" Peter shouted even louder hoping to drown out the voices in his head.

Everyone was quiet. Only the sound of the fire cackled at his feet. No one knew what to say. Peter wanted to run and hide. He felt backed into a corner with no escape.

Tick. Tick. Tick. An hour passed. It seemed like an eternity, when finally another man whispered. "Certainly this fellow was with Him for he is a Galilean." The whisper seemed as loud as a Tribune's command to his Legion of soldiers.

Peter grabbed his own head and shook it with all of his might—"I don't know HIM!"

Cock-a-doodle-doo.

The sound of the rooster sliced the atmosphere.

Weeks from now, this same Peter would appear boldly before all of his Jewish brethren on the steps of the temple, proclaiming with courage and conviction, the belief in the death and resurrection of Jesus. But now, all eyes were locked on him as he buried his head in his hands—tears streaming down his face. He could hide his face, but he could not hide his failure.

I had looked at him as we passed, but he could not bear to look at Me. "*Look* at Me, Peter. *Look* at Me. I love you. I told you before it came to pass that you might believe." I silently whispered under my breath.

I had said to him...

"The Son of man will be betrayed into the hands of men.
They will kill Me, but on the third day, I will rise again."

Luke 24:7

As I passed, I prayed he would remember these words I had said...
"These things I have spoken unto you, that in me you might have peace.
In the world ye shall have tribulation: but be of good cheer;
I have overcome the world." John 16:33

Believe, Peter, *believe.*

I wept for Peter, my beloved Peter, as he denied me, just as I weep for you when you have denied Me—for the times you will deny Me still—for the times when the lies wash over the truth— to the point you are drowning in the sea of your own failure.

It is at this moment I died for you— for I am thinking of you, as I am thinking of Peter running away from his moment of truth. He would need a scapegoat, one who could take the blame for his misdeeds or errors. On the Day of Atonement the chief priest would symbolically lay the sins of the people upon a goat which was sent alive into the wilderness, a scapegoat. Peter needed a scapegoat, an atonement for his sin, just as you need a scapegoat. I am that scapegoat.

And now, the ultimate Day of Atonement had come, I must finish the work I was sent here to do—to take the sins of all of humanity upon Myself—for My Father in heaven requires atonement from sin and I, the Lamb of God, have come as a scapegoat to make reconciliation for the sins of the people. I knew Peter would need My forgiveness, just as I know you would need My forgiveness. It is why I proceed these early morning hours to appear before Pilate, surrounded by the Pharisees and Sadducees of the temple and the Roman soldiers. I must atone for Peter, as I must atone for you—

"Though your sins are as scarlet, they will be white as snow." Isaiah 1:18

Though you forsake Me. I will not forsake you. It was for Peter, one of my closest followers, that I had to continue My journey to the cross. It was for you… It is for you…

I kept walking, shedding drops of blood as I walked—each step I took towards obedience unto death, death on a cross—I was overcoming the world, darkness and satan, himself, for all time—for after all, I was thinking of you, as I am thinking of you now…

I pray for you in your hour of doubt, when you think the dark night of your soul will never end—when the dawn breaks to find you denying the very One who died for you. When the rooster of human frailty crows, I am *still* with you. I have never left you. I died for you, because I love you.

Tomorrow you will be a living stone to fit perfectly in My heavenly kingdom if you stop. Turn around. Look at Me.

Believe.

For I am praying for you, that your faith will *not* fail—for I am thinking of you.

Setting...
En Route to Pilate: Jesus the Good Shepherd

John 10:1-18

"A hired hand will run away when the life of the sheep
Are threatened, because he does not own the sheep.
When he sees a wolf coming, he leaves the sheep and flees.
The wolf catches the sheep and scatters them.
The hired hand flees because he does not care about the sheep."

"I am the good shepherd; and I know My sheep, and am known
By My own. As the Father knows Me, even so I know the Father;
And I lay down My life for the sheep.
And other sheep I have which are not of this fold; them also I must bring,
and they will hear My voice;
And there will be one flock and one shepherd."

A good shepherd will risk his own life for the safety of the sheep.

Everyone who had said they loved Me had now run away. But I am the Good Shepherd. The wolves in sheep's clothing walked next to Me. Dressed in priestly robes and garments. There will always be those who say they are righteous, but are not.

My sheep *know* My voice. You can *know* Me. You never need to be deceived by the voice of a false shepherd. You will know a false leader by their fruits.

"Beware of false prophets, who come to you in sheep's clothing,
But inwardly they are ravenous wolves.
You will know them by their fruits.
Do men gather grapes from thorn bushes or figs from thistles?
Even so, every good tree bears good fruit, but a bad tree bears bad fruit.

A good tree cannot bear bad fruit, nor can a bad tree bear good fruit.
Every tree that does not bear good fruit is cut down and thrown into the
fire. Therefore by their fruits you will know them.
Matthew 7:15-20
"The fruit of the Spirit is love, joy, peace, patience, kindness,
goodness, faithfulness." Galatians 5:22-23

If a shepherd exudes these good attributes, he or she has the qualities of a good leader. If he or she does not bear these attributes. FLEE.

The Good Shepherd will not lose *one* of His sheep. I, as the Good Shepherd, will move heaven and earth to find just *one* of My lost lambs. Each lamb is precious to Me. You are precious to Me.

My sheep listen to My voice; I know them, and they follow Me.
I give them eternal life, and they will never perish. No one can snatch them
out of My hand. My Father who has given them to Me is greater than all.
No one can snatch them out of My Father's hand...."
John 10:27-29

Many false shepherds will feed themselves. They will try to control the My sheep. They will scream at them, condemn them, criticize them, make them feel guilty, and gain wealth from their offerings. They will tell My sheep that they, the shepherds, are the only ones who can interpret the scriptures. False shepherds will tell the sheep that they cannot interpret the scriptures for themselves. They will also tell My people teach false doctrines, even doctrines of devils.

"Woe, shepherds of Israel who have been feeding themselves! Should not the shepherds feed the flock? You eat the fat and clothe yourselves with the wool, you slaughter the fat sheep without feeding the flock. Those who are sickly you have not strengthened, the diseased you have not healed, the broken you have not bound up, the scattered you have not brought back, nor have you sought for the lost; but with force and with severity you have dominated them...." *Ezekiel 34:3-4*

"I am the Good Shepherd
and I know My sheep, every one, by name and it is this night,
I lay My life down for you, for you are the lambs of My Father's flock.
You are the sheep of His hand and the people of His pasture.
His love for you caused Him to send His very own Son to die for you and it
is because of this love for you, I will lay my life down..."
John 10 (paraphrased)

For I was thinking of you, as I am thinking of you now...

In case "any man spoil you through philosophy and vain deceit, after the tradition of men, after the rudiments of the world, and not after the simplicity found in Jesus." *Colossians 2:8*

I am the Good Shepherd continuing My journey this night, to be hung on a cross, innocent. I will confront every false shepherd, every false doctrine, every false teaching, false preaching, false prophet, false god, and lying wolf in sheep's clothing. In my Truth, I will crush their lies forever.

"For in Me dwells all the fullness of the Godhead bodily;
You are complete in Me, who is the head of all principality and power."
Colossians 2:9 1

I have loved you and known you since before you were born. I have written your name on My heart. I have created you to have intimate fellowship with My Father, your Creator, to live in peace with nature and harmony with others.

"I know when you get up and sit down.
I understand your thoughts from afar.
I am with you on your path and near you when you lie down.
I am acquainted with all your ways.
There is not a word on your tongue that I don't already know.
I protect you and have laid My hand upon you.
There is nowhere you can flee from My Spirit.
If you take the wings of the morning and dwell in the far side of the sea,
Even there, My hand will lead you, surely My hand will hold you.
Darkness will not consume you.
Even the night will be light around you.
The darkness and the light are the same to Me.
I formed your inward parts and covered you in your mother's womb.
You are fearfully and wonderfully made.
Your tiny body was not hid from Me, when you were made in secret.
My works are marvelous. I have fashioned your days.
If you would count the precious thoughts I have for you,
They are more than the number of grains of sand.
When you wake, I am still with you..."
Psalm 139 (Paraphrased)

I will help you in time of need and never let you go. I will look for you across the sea. I will long for you on the waters. I will be with you on the high mountain worshipping Me. I will rescue you in the lonely valley below, when you are in despair. I am not found in religious walls, nor spires tall. I am the Lamb of God who would die for one, even if it is only for you.

I know your hurt. I can see your pain. For I am a man unlike any other. I am God in flesh, here to breathe life into you. I am calling, calling, calling to you. If you will *listen,* you will hear My voice. I speak with the gentle soft whisper of the Good Shepherd who will lead you to the end of the age and beyond. I will never leave of forsake you.

My voice is not in the wind, nor in the earthquake, as I said to Elijah at Mount Horeb...

"And behold, the LORD was passing by!
And a great and strong wind was rending the mountains
And breaking in pieces the rocks before the LORD;
But the LORD was not in the wind.
And after the wind an earthquake,
But the LORD was not in the earthquake.
After the earthquake a fire, but the LORD was not in the fire;
And after the fire—a sound—of a still, small voice."
I Kings 19:11,12

You have to be *quiet* to listen.

"Come unto Me all you who are weary and are heavy-laden.
Come to Me and find rest for your soul."
Matthew 11:28

If anyone comes to Me, I will in no way cast them out.

I am aware of you when you are searching. I am in tune with your deepest longings. I know your hopes and dreams. I have never wanted harm to come to you. The world is in a fallen state since the fall of Adam and Eve, but I have come to redeem you—to take you to My Father's house.

"Let not your heart be troubled; you believe in God,
Believe also in Me.
In My Father's house are many mansions;
If it were not so, I would have told you.
I go to prepare a place for you.
And if I go and prepare a place for you,
I will come again and receive you to Myself;

That where I am, there you may be also.
And where I go you know, and the way you know."
John 14:1-4
"Peace I leave with you, my peace I give to you: not as the world gives,
Give I to you. Let not your heart be troubled, neither let it be afraid."
John 14:27
"And now I have told you before it comes to pass,
That, when it comes to pass, you might believe."
John 14:29

Those walking beside Me, enslaving Me in chains, condemning Me with their religious ideas, do not know Me. But you can *know* Me. Each of you can know Me, on an individual basis. Call upon Me, I will give you a new heart for I long for fellowship with you, for I was thinking of you, as I am thinking of you now...

"My sheep know My voice
And it is those who belong to Me who follow Me.
I am the door.
All those who have ever come before Me or after Me
Are thieves and robbers.
I am the door.
If any one enters in, he or she will be saved..."
John 10:9-16

The doors of spiritual darkness appear to be so open, so free, adorned with temptations—promises of desires and deep longings to be met. Some are beautiful looking doors—leading to riches, fame, and success. Even doors of religious studies can be a dead end if you do not take the time to *know* Me. You can tuck me away or neatly hide My word in dusty shelves bursting with volumes of doctrines, but doctorates and Phd's won't get you in heaven's gates. Only a relationship with *Yahweh* through Me, the Door of the Sheep, will secure you a place in heaven. The union with Me is a living, breathing, dynamic, daily encounter with the Living God. You may look good in the eyes of others, but your reputation with Me, your Lord and your God, is all that matters.

"Did you know, that I hide the true wisdom from the wise
And deliver it unto babes?" Matthew 11:25

You may need to ask yourself—what do you need to leave behind to follow Me?

"For the door is narrow and few there be who will find it. The door to destruction is wide and many there will be that pursue this path."
Mathew 7:13-14

The two paths lead to two separate places. One day, the light will separate from the dark forever. There will be no way to keep it together. Light will go into light. Dark will go into dark, when the heavens roll back like a scroll. *Isaiah 34:4; Revelation 6:14*

"Many will come in that day and say, 'Lord, Lord, didn't we do many mighty wonderful works in your name?' and I will say to them..."
"Depart from Me. I never knew you."
Matthew 24:5

As the Good Shepherd, I lay My life down, that I may take it up again. A God who loves you, is a God who would die for you. A Good Shepherd lays His life down for the sheep.

"Therefore My Father loves Me,
Because I lay down My life that I may take it again.
No one takes it from Me, but I lay it down of Myself.
I have power to lay it down, and I have power to take it again.
This command I have received from My Father."
John 10:18

As the men in priestly robes led Me to be sentenced, I felt the burden of a day in the future, when they, themselves, would stand before My Father, and be sentenced. I thought of how these priests will answer, when My Father asks them how they treated His Son. What will they say? Will they be silent as I am now?

I will remain silent.

What keeps Me treading this narrow path, My face marred and disfigured—in pain and humility—counted as a thief, a liar, a false prophet, and a fool—is you.

I humbled Myself in the form of a servant, fashioned Myself as a man, became obedient to death—to die even on a cross, a Roman execution stake—for I was thinking of you, as I am thinking of you now...

When you have locked yourself behind closed doors; when your greed, your lust, or your sinful acts are too dark to mention in the light of day; when, like Peter, your reputation is ruined and there is nowhere to hide; when the entrance to your soul is locked behind ludicrous lies that entangled you in a web of deceit; when the doors of *your will*, not Mine, have slammed in your face and you have lost the key to be free or perhaps even the strength to push the right door open; when you have slammed the door in My face, in order to hide in your sin, due to hardness of heart, sadness, grief and disappointment—it is at this moment, I, the Door of the sheep, the Good Shepherd—am thinking of you...

I *am* the Door, when there is no door. I am the Door from heaven and to heaven—the Door that appears from seemingly nowhere, because it is so simple to open. Yet the answer has been in existence from before time began. The Door, leading to eternal life, is found in your *one* choice, made in humility.

"Behold, I stand at the door of your heart and knock.

If you hear My voice, open the door. I will come into you..."

I will come *into* the depths of your destruction, into the crevices of your heart, into the shut-off, locked-up places of your deepest sorrows. When I enter in, I will breathe life into your lifeless, tired, worn out prison cell of your solitary confinement—

"...I will come in and dine with you and you with Me."

Revelation 3:20

I am the Door who heals. The Door who restores. The Door who waits for you to turn the key of your heart, to say yes to the Lamb of God, the Savior of the whole world, the Savior who longs for you, waits for you—the Savior who, this dark night, is pressing on to the early morning hours—thinking of you.

As I walk with the cohort of Roman Soldiers, led by a Roman *Chiliarch*, a commander of one thousand soldiers, along with the servants from the palace of the high priest and the leaders of the temple, as My people Israel are sleeping, anticipating the Passover, the Living Passover, the Door to the Holy of Holies of the Temple, is being opened to save the world. Anyone who enters in this Door will be saved and I will remember you before My Father in heaven.

Open the Door... I am thinking of you...

Setting...
Jesus passes Judas on the way to appear before Pilate

Luke:22:1-21; Matthew 4:1-11

I felt as if this night would never end, as I walked, bound with chains, to be sentenced to death before Pilate. Every second seemed an eternity, as I was being led as a Lamb to the slaughter. A fragment of my former self, after having endured grueling hours being falsely accused in the court of Sanhedrin, I noticed Judas, lurking in the shadows near Me. He seemed shocked by the chains that held Me captive.

He, of course, had chains wrapped around him, but was unaware of them. The shackles had been tethered to him by his own choices. I had not forgotten him. I loved him.

I had formed him in his mother's womb. I knew the exact number of hairs on his head, just as I know the number of each hair on your head.

"Are not two sparrows sold for a farthing
And one of them shall not fall on the ground without your Father.
The very hairs of your head are all numbered.
Fear not therefore, you are of more value than many sparrows."
Matthew 10:30

I knew each thought and intention of his heart, just as I know each thought and intention of your heart. Judas had never left My thoughts for a moment. My thoughts toward him were more than the grains of sand spread across the beaches of the earth.

Judas thought I had forgotten him, but I could not forget him? How could I forget one of My own of Israel, My first born son? I had engraved the people of Israel on the palms of My hands. *Isaiah 49:16*

Judas's palms were pulsating with sweat. He *wished* he could forget. Oh, how Judas wished he could forget—but how can one forget a deliberate act of betrayal? The guilt and shame he carried were more tangible than the sweat on his palms. How can one forget a crime — a crime of the worst kind — a betrayal of the heart?

My heart wept as I saw him standing there watching Me in the outer court of the Palace of Caiaphas. My heart began to break for Judas, as it would later break on the cross, pouring out blood and water — just as My heart breaks for you when you are hiding in the shadows of your sin.

Judas felt his heart split at this moment, too; not with empathy and compassion like My heart, but with a sinking feeling of deep, deep regret — an irreparable fracture, like the sound of thin ice cracking beneath his feet as he was walking in the middle of a frozen lake. Remorse set into the depth of his being like gangrene spreads into an infection.

His mind raced back to the events that had led to the moment of his betrayal of Me. He had convinced himself that he was doing the "right" thing. Fear and suspicion had begun to surround Me. He had not only heard the priests openly condemning Me, but he had overheard talk in the streets regarding conspiracies of putting Me to death. He was afraid for his own life. But he was more afraid of public opinion, because he wasn't sure who he was. He teetered between two opinions.

If he could have just believed who I was, it would have given him a stronger sense of himself and his own worth. If he could have believed that My kingdom was not of this earth, he might have held onto the small bit of faith he had, in order to gain his reward in heaven.

I thought of My own time of testing, My forty days of temptation, in the Judean wilderness. A lifeless, virtually unending sea, of sand dunes surrounded Me. The sun blazed through the vast blue sky. The heat of the desert, rising through My sandals, was nothing compared to an eternity spent without God in the heat of hell. I needed to face the heat of satan's fire, in order to be victorious — for you.

For I was thinking of you, as I am thinking of you now...

The Spirit had led me into the wilderness, to be tempted by satan, before My ministry would begin on Earth. I fasted for forty days and forty nights. The hunger and thirst I experienced were beyond any agony I had ever felt in my flesh as a man, but I knew that the fasting would help Me to overcome the temptations. I needed to be strong in the Spirit.

Being comfortable in the flesh does not arm a person with the spiritual strength to fight the biggest battles. Many of My people over time will be comfortable and even complacent in their lives to the point of incompetence. When the enemy comes to devour, they will not be able to resist. They will not have the strength to fight. My weapons are not in the flesh, but in the spirit. The flesh needs to be fed less, in order for the spirit to be strong.

"Be sober, be vigilant; because your adversary the devil walks about like a roaring lion, seeking whom he may devour." *I Peter 5:8*

I endured the temptation of the wilderness, so that when you are in your own wilderness of temptation, you will know you have a Savior—a high priest who can understand and sympathize with the feeling of your weaknesses; and was tempted in all points, yet without sin.

When the tempter came to Me, I was spiritually prepared.

Satan said, "If You are the Son of God, command that these stones become bread."

When I answered him, I quoted from the word of God. I did not try to reason with him, argue with him, or engage him in a conversation. I answered and said, *"It is written, 'Man shall not live by bread alone, but by every word that proceeds from the mouth of God.'"*

When you are in your own time of temptation, do not attempt to answer with your own thoughts, but respond only with My name and with the word of God.

Next, the devil took Me up to the Holy City, Jerusalem, and set Me on a pinnacle of the temple. "If You are the Son of God, throw Yourself down. For it is written: 'He shall give His angels charge over you, and in their hands they shall bear you up, lest you dash your foot against a stone.'"

This is where temptation gets tricky. Satan might use the word of God to test you to do something that is not in line with the character of God; perhaps it seems like a good idea, but it is at an inappropriate time or place. This is where you need to *know* your God. Know the character of God and study to know the word of God in its entirety. A scripture, taken out of context can be used for someone's personal gain, and can tempt you to do something you know is not right.

I said to satan firmly, *"It is written, 'You shall not put the Lord you God to the test.'"*

Again, the devil took Me up on an exceedingly high mountain, and showed Me all the kingdoms of the world and their glory. And he said to

Me, "All these things I will give You if You will fall down and worship me."

I said to him, *"Away with you, satan! For it is written, 'You shall worship the Lord your God, and shall serve Him only.'"*

Then the devil left Me, and angels came and ministered to Me.

I knew My Father in heaven, whom I served.

"I do what my Father tells me to do
So that the people of the world may know that I love My Father."

John 14:31

I knew the heavenly kingdom was not of this earth; therefore, when satan tempted Me with temporary worldly power and fame, I was able to stand and resist him.

That fateful moment, less than twenty-four hours ago, when Judas had made his decision to betray Me, when the adversary, satan, had entered him, was not the pivotal moment of his decision. No. Judas had opened a door to satan days before, perhaps even months before.

When had Judas opened the door of his heart to the adversary? Was it in a moment of greed? Was it motivated from fear that I might be put on trial and he would be punished along with Me? Did he want to be famous or accepted by the teachers of the *Torah*?

The act of betraying Me, his Messiah, for thirty pieces of silver— *Why*? *How* did it happen? Had satan been knocking at the door of his mind, of his heart, and of his soul for a long time? Had the adversary been whispering in his ear for months?

Did Judas have a heart of crime from the beginning when he decided to follow his Messiah or did he take a wrong turn at some point on the journey? For, indeed, this is a journey of free choice.

Through fear, greed, and a desire to please men, he had opened the door to satan, little by little.

Judas' primary choice to let satan in was a choice made of free will, but now—*who* was doing the choosing? Had Judas become a slave to the adversary, the devil, the hater of his soul?

"Would you like to know how to locate *Yeshua*? I may be able to find him for you..." Judas had said to the chief priests. "What are you willing to give me if I hand Him over to you?" *Mathew 26:15*

Satan had entered Judas just as he had entered the serpent in the Garden of Eden.

As Judas gazed upon Me bound in My chains of obedience unto death, I saw him bound in his own chains of disobedience to God resulting in his decision to betray Me—just as I see you, perhaps bound in your own chains—trapped in a decision to let satan in—the moment you sold your soul for thirty pieces of silver to betray your Lord.

"Oh, it was not thirty pieces of silver," you might say, "and I would never betray my Lord." But you may have betrayed Me for one cheap night of pleasured company with someone you should not have been with. Your thirty pieces of silver may have been secret acts of robbing money or goods, or even robbing the innocence of another. You might think you could have never been as Judas; after all, who could be worse than the one who betrayed his Messiah, the Son of God, for only thirty pieces of silver? Yet, you may have betrayed Me with one kiss and do not even have the silver coins left to contribute to the temple.

Judas felt the silver in this girdle—cumbersome, clinking coins clanging together as he slithered in the shadows. At the same time, the shackles choking his soul were like snakes encircling his heart—hissing at him with fanged jaws, in the early morning air.... "Guilty! Guilty!"

Surely, everyone could hear the blood money shrieking in his pouch. Surely, everyone near him *knew*—he was the man—he was the man —*he* was the man who betrayed JESUS.

A few short hours ago, he stole away from the supper, leaving his spiritual brothers, John, James, Peter, Philip, Luke, Mark, Thomas, Andrew, Jude, James, son of Alphaeus, and Judas, son of Simon. He *had* to leave, because of the smell of the lamb, the *Pesachal* lamb, the symbol of the saving blood of the passover was too strong.

Judas had never felt so restless. His throat tightened up. He had trouble breathing. He started gasping for air as the smell of the lamb filled the upper room. He felt quite ill as he heard Me say to My Disciples...

"I have so looked forward to sharing this Passover with you...
I tell you, that from now on I will not celebrate it again
Until it has been given its full meaning in the Kingdom of God."
Luke 22:15
As I took the third cup of wine, I made this blessing,
"Take this and drink it together, for I tell you,
I will not drink this wine again until the Kingdom of God comes.
This cup is the new covenant of the God of Israel,

sealed and ratified by My blood, which is being poured out for you..."
Luke 22:20

The blood! The blood! Judas could smell the blood in his nostrils. Satan who had entered him hated this blood—this was the blood of the New Covenant—the *B'rit Hadashah,* which would finally nullify satan's devious act of temptation to Eve and Adam in the Garden of Eden—the blood that would open the gates to eternal fellowship with God.

Satan screamed inside of Judas, but Judas could not open his mouth. He felt putrefying vomit rising in his throat—his body was writhing and reeling—his skin crawling.

At this split second, Judas felt he, himself, would split in two. He felt all of hell unleashed inside of him as his eyes darted about the large room upstairs in the house of Mark. He could not remember how he got to this point of his life. He could not trace back to the moment he had let the adversary in.

Had not he once believed in his Messiah Jesus and would have given his life for him? So why? How did he end up being the one to betray the Messiah? Yet he knew he was the one, for he had made the decision— little by little—step by step. One more step into the darkness. One more step for gain. Another tiptoe with trepidation into fear. One more coin counted for greed. One more for self-preservation—until finally, he had submitted wholly and absolutely to satan, the deceiver of the brethren, who had but one plan—to kill the Messiah, the chosen one of God.

Satan planned to stamp out God forever so that he could be worshipped as god, just as he demanded to be worshipped as god when he was an angelic being in heaven. He was cast out by Michael, the magnificent archangel of God, who worships God and only God, and fights for God's people of Israel and the Israel of God—night and day.

"The man who will betray Me is here at the table with Me,"
I had said to My disciples "Woe to the man by whom Jesus is betrayed!
It would have been better for him if he had not been born."
Mathew 26:21;24

"Ahhhhhhhhh!" Judas cried out when he heard these words. He did not realize he was not at all in control anymore, as the adversary overcame him. He had said yes to the serpent willingly, but now the lying serpent who had been cursed to crawl on his belly encircled Judas, inside and out. Judas, a Jewish man from Judea, an Israelite, one of God's chosen disciples, had chosen to serve the serpent instead. And now, the serpent could not save him.

I knew what Judas was doing—just as I know the choices you have made, choices you are making now, and the ones you will be making in the future. You may have opened doors, little by little, to listen to satan's lies. You may have even made that decision to serve the creature rather than the creator—to enter into a covenant with the prince of darkness—to sell your very own soul to him for fame or fortune. Now, the coins of blood money are jingling in *your* pocket and the chains of the snake are coiled around *your* throat. You might be choking, gasping for air, hoping to be freed— when you realize, as Judas did, in the deepest part of his being, "I have betrayed My Lord, My Messiah, the Savior of the whole world."

"Fear not! I have overcome the world." John 16:33

I have come to buy you back. It is not too late. As long as you have breath—call out to Me. Repent. Turn to Me and live. My blood can redeem your soul. One drop of My blood ransoms your soul from the gates of hell. With My blood, I will write your name in My book of Life.

Judas looked at Me once more before frantically stumbling away. Not with the secretive look of betrayal and deceit he had at the Passover earlier. This time it was a look of despair.

"What can I do?" I heard him screaming in his head.

Judas ran from Me but you can come to Me. You can find forgiveness. For I was thinking of you, as I am thinking of you now...

Setting...
En Route to Pilate, Judas flees from Jesus

Matthew 27:1-10

As Judas fled into the night, helter-skelter, My eyes looked upon him one last time. I could feel his heart wildly beating. Satan had left his body now. His nasty work was over. He had been invited into Judas and once Judas had done his bidding, satan tossed him by the side of the road, just as he has done and will do to any pawn who says yes to his hideous schemes— Judas could once again feel the beat of his own heart, even if he did not want to.

Baboom! Baboom! His heart pounded in his chest. Surely, his heart beat so fiercely it burst through his chest. He was breathing hysterically. His lungs were on fire. He felt his lungs would rupture with cries of guilt. Even if he tried to silence his lungs, they would scream—"You are guilty! You are guilty!"

He felt his bowels would spill out onto the ground, gushing forth, seeping with stench, and rotting with fear—the fear of guilt—fear of being found out. He felt his eyes had rolled back in his head, examining himself. He felt every other eye near him penetrating into his being. Surely, all eyes saw his shame, looking deep within him, into the depths of his heart.

"But no one knows who I am," he tried to comfort himself, smooth his sweat-drenched, wrinkled garment. But the secret of the thirty pieces of silver, the secret of handing over his Messiah, his Savior, his Lord, seemed to be spilling out of his psyche onto the barren road. Even though it was nighttime, surely every eye could see his secret, too damning to be contained.

Judas knew I had seen him, as I stumbled past him, being yanked harshly forward by the Roman guards. He had witnessed the crowds of people who were gathering to see the pandemonium as I was leaving the assembly in the High Priest's palace. Even though he felt the eyes of the crowd on him, he was aware of My Presence more than anything else.

Even though My back was turned to him now, He could feel the eternal eyes of My Presence searing into his soul. I was still thinking of him.

His secret had made him a slave. He was bound, he was gagged, he was ridiculed and mocked, by his decision to betray his Lord. Just as you are bound and gagged, silenced in the dark crevices of your soul where you keep your secrets buried.

"Guilt! Guilt!" The secrets won't stay quiet, "Guilt! Guilt!" The secrets refuse to stay hidden in their tomb any longer. The secrets are turning on you, exposing themselves to others—through your eyes. The windows to your soul are open for all the world to see, but more disarming than the eyes of humanity peering into your soul are the flaming eyes of a holy and righteous God.

"I am the Alpha and Omega, the First and the Last, the One
In the midst of seven gold menorahs, clothed with a robe down to My feet,
With a gold band around My chest, hair as white as wool,
As white as snow, with eyes as a flame of fire.
My feet, refined brass as if they burned in a furnace,
With My voice as the sound of many waters.
In My right hand are seven stars and out of My mouth goes
a sharp two-edged sword and My face shines as the sun in full strength."
Revelation 1:8;13-15

Like Judas, My sacrifice is your only hope for eternal salvation on the day when the deep secrets of your heart are unveiled in the Presence of *Adonai*. The Presence of God which Moses felt at the burning bush was too sacred and holy to be witnessed by pure mortals. Even the chosen deliverer, Moses, had to remove the sandals from his feet as he was standing on holy ground.

A priest entering into the Holy of Holies, in the temple, would wear bells on the bottom of his robe attached to a rope in case his heart or his sacrifice was not acceptable to God, either of which would cause him to die instantly in the Presence of God. If this was the case, he would be pulled out by the rope. No one else would dare to enter in. As long as the bells could be heard, those outside of the Holy of Holies knew that God had accepted the sacrifice of the priest and he was still alive.

The day when bells cease to ring, when you have come into the Presence of *Adonai* and you hear nothing but ominous silence, along with the beating of your own heart—and you realize that each person must stand before God alone—no one will be with you—not your sister nor your mother, not your father nor your brother, not your priest nor your rabbi, nor the persons in your synagogue or in your church; not your teacher, your president, the government, not even your husband or wife—only you, exposed before a Holy and Righteous God.

Judas felt exposed as he looked at Me bound and chained. He frantically grabbed at his tunic to see if he was still clothed, just as Adam and Eve grabbed for a fig leaf when the Lord God visited them in the garden after they had eaten the forbidden fruit. They felt naked in the Garden having felt shame for the first time, when they knew they had sinned against God. In the same way, Judas knew now—he had sinned against God.

"I have sinned! I have betrayed an innocent man to death!" The words clamored inside his mind, just as each silver coin clamored in his girdle. Each coin now felt extremely weighty, as if each one had become a millstone attached to a cord wrapped around his neck.

He remembered seeing Me surrounded by the little children who came to see Me.

"Let the children come to Me."

I said to him...

"Any one who causes one of these innocent ones to stumble, it is better for a millstone to be tied around his neck and cast into the sea."

Matthew 18:6

A millstone can weigh up to 3000 pounds. Now Judas felt he had thirty millstones tied to his neck. A vast ocean loomed before him, an endless abyss where evil ones who hurt the innocent are cast into—forever and ever.

"I have betrayed innocent blood!" Judas was certain every person near him could hear his harsh whisper rasping again in his throat. Judas blood pumped hot. It pulsed through every vein and artery. Each cell of his blood now felt tainted with sin.

He did not know that one drop of My blood, the blood of His Messiah, His Lord, could save his soul. One drop could make him whole again. One drop could sever the cords of his guilt, loose the heavy weights from around his neck and cleanse his blood from sin.

No—Judas was not aware of anything but his own blood. His own neck. The evidence of the coins clanking in his pouch and the feeling of being utterly absolutely alone. He was aware of only one—himself. He knew what he had done... just as you know what you have done. Remorse sets in, when you realize you have said or done something so horribly awful or selfish—you cannot take it back and you have to deal with the consequences of your sin.

"Oh, but I have not committed a hideous crime," you may say. "I have not betrayed my Savior as Judas did."

> *"Truly, I say to you, as you did it to one of the least of these,*
> *My brothers, you did it to Me."*
> *Matthew 25:40*

Each of your thoughts and actions will be taken into account when you die and stand before the Judgment seat of God. A whisper of gossip here. A simple betrayal of trust there. A dishonest wage gained in secret.

"When I come in My glory and all the angels with Me, ...I will separate people, one from one another as the shepherd separates the sheep from the goats; and I will put the sheep on My right and the goats on the left."

> *"Then I will say to those on My right, 'Come, you who are blessed*
> *Of My Father, inherit the kingdom prepared for you from the foundation*
> *Of the world. For I was hungry, and you gave Me something to eat;*
> *I was thirsty, and you gave Me something to drink; I was a stranger,*
> *And you invited Me in; naked, and you clothed Me;*
> *I was sick, and you visited Me; I was in prison, and you came to Me.'"*
> *"Then the righteous will answer Me, 'Lord, when did we see You hungry*
> *And feed You, or thirsty and give You something to drink?*
> *And when did we see You a stranger and invite You in,*
> *Or naked and clothe You? When did we see You sick, or in prison,*
> *And come to You?' I will answer and say to them,*
> *'Truly I say to you, to the extent that you did it to one of these brothers*
> *Of Mine, even the least of them, you did it to Me.'"*
> *"Then I will also say to those on My left, 'Depart from Me, accursed ones,*
> *into the eternal fire which has been prepared for the devil and his angels;*
> *For I was hungry, and you gave Me nothing to eat; I was thirsty, and you*
> *gave Me nothing to drink; I was a stranger, and you did not invite Me in;*
> *Naked, and you did not clothe Me;*

sick, and in prison, and you did not visit Me.'"

"Then they themselves also will answer, 'Lord, when did we see
You hungry, or thirsty, or a stranger, or naked, or sick, or in prison,
And did not take care of You?'"

"I will answer them, 'Truly I say to you, to the extent
That you did not do it to one of the least of these, you did not do it to Me.'
These will go away into eternal punishment,
but the righteous into eternal life."

Matthew 25:31-45 (Paraphrased)

"But I have been a good person!" You might interject. But what about the acts you have committed in your heart?

"He who says he is walking in the light, but hates his brother,
Is in darkness even now... He who hates his brother or sister is a murderer
and you know that no murderer has eternal life abiding in him or her."

I John 3:15

"If you look on a woman or man to lust after her or him in your
heart, you have committed adultery already."

Matthew 5:27-28

At the dead-end street of your guilt, the realization of a crime committed with no way to reverse the act and no way to take it back—it is at this moment when the intentions of your heart are exposed, when you, like Judas, are drowning in the pool of your own perspiration of self-degeneration—you seek only self-preservation—it is at this time you must know you have a Savior—a Savior who does not preserve Himself, but who gives His life freely to preserve *you*. A Savior who sweat great drops of blood for you, who aches for you, cries for you, makes penance for you.

I, Jesus, your Messiah, the spotless lamb of God...will continue this path of salvation for you this day, bound and chained as a criminal so that you, as a criminal, bound by the crimes of your heart and locked in the chains of your past—when the sinking guilt in your deepest being shrieks out your harsh reality, "O wretched man or woman that I am. Who can save me from this body of death?" *Romans 7:24-25*

Call upon Me. I can set you free. I have prayed for you. I will die for you today because I love you. I know you have sinned and fallen short of the glory of God. I was thinking of you, as I am thinking of you now...

"All of you like sheep have gone astray,
each of person has turned to his own way;

But the LORD has caused the iniquity of humanity to fall on Me.
I was oppressed and I was afflicted, Yet I did not open My mouth.
Like a lamb that is led to slaughter,
And like a sheep that is silent before its shearers,
So I did not open My mouth."
Isaiah 53:6,7
"I was taken away and not one of my generation protested against
My death. I was cut off from the land of the living for the crimes of the
people who deserved their own punishment.
I was buried with the wicked.
Although I had done no violence nor did I speak any wicked or deceitful
words, yet it pleased Adonai to bruise Me
To present Me as a guilt offering.
Therefore, I poured out My soul unto death.
I was numbered and counted as a criminal. I bore the sins of many..."
Isaiah 53:8-10

When Judas was seized with this remorse, he had a brief encounter with clarity. He reached for the thirty pieces of silver in his pouch. "I will take them back! I will take them back to the head C*ohanim*. I must take them back! Perhaps I can undo what I have done!"

He scrambled madly. He bull-dozed his way through the curious crowds as he frantically sought out the chief priests and elders, the same ones who had handed him the silver pieces, less than twenty-four hours ago. He remembered their faces. When he found them, he cried out, "I have sinned! I have betrayed innocent blood!"

The priests stared at Judas, stone faced and cold, hiding safely in a group. Each one poked his head out of the gaggle for split second to gaze upon the spectacle with curiosity, but then quickly ducked again, ashamedly bobbing their heads in front and then behind each other, much like a pack of rats, squinting from a bright light. It is much easier to hide between the lines of opinions of others, than it is to stand alone.

Judas, on the other hand, had come to the stark realization of his aloneness and the responsibility of the decisions of his soul. This feeling of being alone was acutely pronounced as he pleaded his case before the assembly of holy men. "I have sinned! I have betrayed innocent blood."

Yes, they had heard what Judas said but the sound traveled no further than the stone wall that surrounded their hearts.

Finally, without even bothering to discuss the matter, they agreed, and shook their heads...

"What is that to us?" They answered—collective, calculated and cold. "That is *your* problem."

They preferred to retain a sense of erroneous virtue and let Judas carry the guilt alone. Judas—knowing his fateful defeat was sealed in their blank wall of insolence, hurled the 30 pieces of silver into the temple sanctuary—and ran.

The pieces of silver dropped near the robes of the priests. As each coin hit the ancient foundation of what was once a holy place, with a ghostly reverberation, it was as if each coin might cause the earth to quake at that very minute and bring the stones of the temple down onto their heads. The priests froze for a moment, as statues, much like the people of Pompeii will look in 70 AD when the lava from the volcanic eruption will turn them to stone in an instance. The priests did not budge an inch, as the coins bounced and rolled, bounced and rolled.

One shiny silver coin rolled right up to the feet of the priests standing in the front. Ironically, it stood on its edge, spinning for what seemed to be an eternity... The priests glared at it, as they might glare at anyone or anything that did not fall in line with their agenda. But the coin glared back as it whirled around, with a violent whirling that sent out a shrill drone, piercing the air with an even greater chill than the coldness of the very hearts within them.

They felt the terror run up their spines of a greater damnation. When the coin stopped, it landed on heads, although the face on the coin was of Caesar, it appeared to them as My face, just for an unearthly second. Of course they imagined this, they thought, as they began to nudge the coins to each other with their feet, hoping to pass the judgment along.

"What do we do with these coins?" One stated as he pushed the coins away from him.

"We cannot put them back in the treasury," another mentioned, with drops of sweat forming on his brow.

"Let us buy a field where we can bury strangers." Another resolved.

"Yes, let's." They decided this in union, as if this decision would wipe the blood from their hands.

Committees, groups, even governments often come to conclusions of such absurdity. Buying a field to bury strangers with the blood money that betrayed their Messiah? Why didn't they just absolve Judas? Why didn't they stop the betrayal before it happened? Do two wrongs make a right?

No, they just passed the coins from one to another and finally to the field called *Haceldama*, which to this day is called the Potter's field, the field of blood. The field had been used to excavate clay for pots. After the clay was removed, such a site would be left unusable for agriculture and thus might as well become a graveyard for those who could not be buried in an orthodox cemetery. Strangers, criminals, and the poor could be conveniently buried in a field already full of trenches and holes.

Of course, what they did not know, but should have known since they had studied the scriptures their whole adult lives, is that their decision to buy the Potter's field fulfilled the prophecy spoken by their own prophet, Jeremiah.

"Then was fulfilled that which was spoken by Jeremiah the prophet, saying, 'And they took the thirty pieces of silver, the price of him that was valued, whom they of the children of Israel did value and gave them for the Potter's Field...'" *Matthew 27:9-10*

"For in Me dwells the fullness of the Godhead.

I am the head of every ruler and authority." Colossians 2:10

Judas had not ultimately sold his Messiah. I had bought Myself as a sacrifice and prophesied it many years earlier so that I could pay the ultimate price—My life—My death on the cross.

When you, like the head priest of the temple, cannot take back the deed which you have done; when you, like Judas, cannot take back the crime you have committed, I have taken this crime on My back. By *My* wounds you are healed. By *My* blood you are forgiven, all you have to do is ask. Ask for forgiveness. No, you cannot take your action back, but I can remember it no more. I am your Messiah, a blood ransom for you, now and forever...

Judas ran and kept running into the cage he had crafted himself. He could have asked forgiveness from Me, but instead, he fled to the Potter's field and hung himself by his own hand. I was thinking of Judas, as I was thinking of you, as I am thinking of you now...

Stop running. Turn around. Come to Me. You can find forgiveness, for I am thinking of you...

Setting…
Right before Jesus enters the Praetorium

Matthew 26:1-13

As the dawn of the day drew near, I knew the agony I had yet to endure. I was not thinking of Judas any longer. The goal set before Me would be to do the will of My Father and give the offering of My life to redeem your soul from death. The eternal life of your soul is My reward. I was thinking of you…

My thoughts turned toward those of you who would deeply love Me and follow Me throughout the years, much like John and Peter. I was thinking of those who would fear Me and speak often of Me. You are My special treasure and the priceless jewels embedded in My crown. I will write your names in My book of remembrance, just as I have written down Mary of Bethany, who anointed Me with precious oil. She is to be remembered whenever the good news is proclaimed.

"Then they that feared the Lord spoke often one to another:
And the Lord hearkened, and heard it, and a book of remembrance
was written before Him for them that feared the Lord,
And that thought upon His name.
And they shall be Mine, saith the Lord of hosts,
in that day when I make up my jewels; and I will spare them,
As a man spares his own son that serves him."
Malachi 3:16-17

My special followers, with soft hearts made pure by My blood, are such stark contrast to Judas and the leaders of the temple, who sought to kill Me. Of course the ones who offered Judas the money were more wicked than Judas. Judas struggled with his choice. He felt guilty afterward. The chief priests and elders, however, were smug in their hierarchy of idolatry and they pridefully thought they were in control of My destiny.

I remembered warning My disciples two days before the Passover...

"The Passover is coming, and I will be handed over to My enemies,
And crucified, nailed to a cross." Matthew 26:2

At that same moment, the head priests and the elders gathered in the palace of Caiaphas, the head priest. As they gathered together, their hearts, like tombstones, spoke to one another like skeletons from the graveyard of their dead religion. They made plans to arrest Me surreptitiously and have Me put to death.

As they were deciding when to arrest Me, "Not during the festival, or the people will riot," they were not cognitive they were constructing another tower of babel—a house doomed to fail—a house of cards. When humans gather together to build a false temple, to worship the creation of their own hands, instead of worshipping the Creator, the building blocks can do nothing but create an unstable building, "For if the Lord does not build the house, the workers build in vain." *Psalms 127:1*

The temple of Solomon was built stone upon stone, for the glory of *Yahuweh* to inhabit it, but now the I, the Messiah, *Yahuweh* in the flesh, was to become the new Temple.

"The times are coming and now are,
That the Father will be worshipped in Spirit and in truth."
John 4:23-24

As I endure the cross, My body will become the Temple, and the temple where the priests and elders gathered will be destroyed.

"Truly I say to you, not one stone here will be left upon another,
which will not be torn down." Matthew 24:2

They reasoned they would mitigate the riot by not arresting me during the festival, but how can one stop the will and timing of *Yahuweh?* How can one stop the leveling of the temple after my death and resurrection?

The temple of Solomon, also called The First Temple, had stood for hundreds of years. The splendor of the temple was unsurpassed. The *Hekhal*, or Holy Place had walls lined with cedar, on which were carved figures of cherubim, palm trees, and open flowers overlaid with gold. The floor of the temple was formed of fir-wood overlaid with gold. The doorposts, of olive-wood, supported folding-doors of fir. The doors of the

Holy of Holies were of olive-wood. On both sets of doors were carved cherubim, palm trees, and flowers, all being overlaid with gold.

I thought of the priests. I thought of each one of them individually. Each one rationalized he was secure in his position. How could this spectacular temple, in which they spent day after day, year after year, be destroyed? If they had only listened and believed Me, their own Messiah, they would have known that the temple they perceived to be so unshakeable would soon be rubble, and that their blind followers would be scattered throughout the Earth for almost two thousand years. If they had listened or believed Me, they may have opened their ears and eyes in order to prepare their followers to receive their Messiah. Instead, their eyes will be blinded until the rise of the Gentile-Church age is fulfilled and they have captured Jerusalem again. Even then, some will still refuse to see.

I had come for My own, but they had not received Me. If they had called out to Me, even now, I would have opened their eyes, but I knew they did not want to see. Their arrogance had blinded them.

I see you, even when you do not want to see Me, even when you need Me desperately, but do not look at Me. I speak in My word and warn of times and seasons, but you do not listen or believe. At these times, I weep for you, as I wept over Jerusalem before the destruction of their temple.

"How often I would have gathered them…
As a mother hen gathers her chicks." Luke 13:34

How often I would gather you under My wings and cover you with My feathers. How I yearn for you to hide in the secret place of the Most High, in the shelter of *El Shaddai,* the Almighty God…

"He that dwells in the secret place of the most High
Shall abide under the shadow of the Almighty.
I will say of the LORD, He is my refuge and my fortress: my God;
In Him will I trust.
Surely He shall deliver thee from the snare of the fowler,
And from the noisome pestilence.
He shall cover thee with His feathers,
And under His wings shalt thou trust:
His truth shall be thy shield and buckler.
Thou shalt not be afraid for the terror by night;
Nor for the arrow that flies by day;

93

Nor for the pestilence that walks in darkness;
Nor for the destruction that wastes at noonday.
A thousand shall fall at thy side, and ten thousand at thy right hand;
But it shall not come nigh thee."

Psalm 91:1-6

If your heart is hard, you cannot see Me nor can you hear Me and perhaps now, you are running blindly in the temple you have built and are finding nothing but rubble. Open your eyes, look at Me. I am the Temple of *Yahuweh*. One look at the compassion in My eyes will cause the crumbling of your temple to cease. You will find a new Temple to dwell in—the Temple of My heart.

"Come to Me if you are weary and heavy laden.
I will give you rest for your soul."

Matthew 11:28

I am thinking of you now, as I was thinking of you then, this morning of the day of my crucifixion.

There is one foundation that will never be moved, never end up in rubble. I am this Stone. The Stone the priests and the elders have rejected will become the cornerstone. I am the Cornerstone in the kingdom of God.

I said to the priests...

"Have you never read in the Scriptures in Psalm 118: 'The stone the builders rejected has become the cornerstone. This is from the Lord, and it is marvelous in our eyes'? Therefore I tell you that the kingdom of God will be taken away from you and given to a people who will produce its fruit. With a humble heart of flesh you can stumble over this stone, fall on Me—confess your brokenness, and be healed. But if the Stone falls on you, in judgment—you will be crushed. Your temple built by your heart of stone will be crushed." *Matthew 21:42-44 (Paraphrased)*

I am now being forcefully shoved by the guards leading me to the Praetorium, Pilate's house, to be presented to Pilate, the Roman Governor. The crowds are gathering not only to see what the commotion is about, but to anticipate the release of a prisoner which is the custom on Passover. One prisoner who is condemned to die will be set free today.

But I was not thinking of Pilate, nor the priests, nor the prisoner... I was thinking of you, just as I am thinking of you now. I had set the plan of my death and resurrection in motion from the beginning of time and I would finish it today—so that when you are halfway through your life and

94

things are not working out exactly the way you had planned, there would still be hope. Hope in Me. I am the author and finisher of your faith. *"Heaven and earth will pass away, but My words will never pass away."*

Matthew 24:35

The door of My house is open to you. In My house you will find mercy and grace. I will continue my course this morning until I have accomplished the plan of salvation for *your* sake. The Temple I am building will never crumble. A builder who sets out to construct a building must count the cost. I have counted the cost for your soul and will purchase your redemption with My own blood. I will finish the journey so when you are weary on your journey, you can count on Me. I will carry you across the finish line if I need to. I am determined to write the end of your story with the blood of My own palms, for I was thinking of you, as I am thinking of you now...

As the guards who seemed to made of steel, yanked My weary body to and fro, I almost lost My goal and vision, and I well very knew...

"Without a vision, one perishes." Proverbs 29:18

At that moment, I heard a bird chirping nearby. Morning had broken. The birds were waking up all around me, a peep here, a tweet there, until a symphony of sweet song filled the ominous air. The enchanting choir, I had created, proved a soothing relief to my ears.

Their welcome sound beckoned Me, coaxing Me to contemplate the creation of the world, the first dawn and the enchantment of the Garden of Eden. Their tiny charming twitters chimed praises to My heavenly Father as I passed. It reminded Me of My celebrated ride on the donkey into Jerusalem, where I was hailed with Palm Branches and shouts of Hosannas, on a week ago—the day I said, that the rocks and stones would surely cry out with their praises, if the tongues around Me would cease.

In the anthem of the birds, I heard the hymn performing the perfect carol of creation and My soul rose to meet daybreak, like the first morning. I was nourished by the purity of My sweet feathered beings and filled with a greater strength to accomplish My purpose, their sweetness elevating My heart before I encountered a noisy crowded Praetorium.

Everything created was perfect—a beautiful world. The only thing ugly—is evil.

The evil that dwelt in the crippled hearts around Me caused Me much anguish. If there were nothing more this morning than this anxious crowd which surrounded Me, it would have been a much more grueling journey. But these birds and these thoughts of My exquisite Garden, caused My soul to harmonize with all of creation.

I was thinking of you, as I am thinking of you now… When you are passing through your own valley of weeping or time of great testing — pause — listen. Spend time in nature, look up at the sky, for…

> *"The heavens declare the glory of God;*
> *And the firmament shows Our craftsmanship.*
> *Day unto day they utter speech, and night unto night they show knowledge.*
> *There is no speech nor language, where their voice is not heard."*
>
> *Psalm 19:1-3*

Look up! For your redemption draws near. For as much evil as there is in the world, there is *more* beauty. For even though there are many people with hard hearts, one heart of pure gold can offer healing, love, and goodness in a time of need.

In a timeless moment, I paused to enter a secret place in My heart, My mind, and My soul, where I tucked away a most poignant memory, which happened only two days ago. It would be the last time I would be able to truly rest before my expedition into hell and back.

A vivid moment, like a sigh, like a breath, like an aroma of perfume, devotion, mixed with the fragrance of unconditional love…

As I lingered at the home of Simon the leper that day, I whispered quietly to My disciples about My upcoming death. Not one of them understood or believed what I meant. Not one.

Mary of Bethany, however, did believe Me. She was present, along with Lazarus, her brother, and Martha, her sister, all of whom were My most beloved friends. As I hung the words of My death in the air, much like piercing the warm and loving atmosphere with a sharp cold knife, Mary overheard my words. When I spoke of My burial, she sensed my wounds were eminent. With an open, trusting heart, she rushed to her cabinet, where she kept her precious oils and flew to My side. She knelt at My feet, and poured out an act of kindness, of worship, and of humility — a devotion to Me which should have melted the hardest of hearts.

I say that it should have, and yet, it didn't. Her actions didn't melt the heart of Judas, who suspiciously watched her open the alabaster box containing the precious perfume. As she poured the ointment on My feet and wiped it with her hair, Judas quickly joined in with the other disciples who were rebuking her act of worship.

They said, "Why this waste?" "This oil could have been sold for a lot of money and given to the poor." They reproached her, not just because the oil was expensive, but because they were in complete denial about My death. They wanted to use the money to build the kingdom on the earth.

I told them...

"For you always have the poor with you;
But you do not always have Me.
For when she poured this perfume on My body,
She did it to prepare Me for burial.
Truly I say to you, wherever this gospel is preached in the whole world,
what this woman has done will also be spoken of in memory of her."
Matthew 11:13

Judas was not as concerned about the poor as he was about the others' approval of him. He cared what others thought and needed their constant reassurance. He had to perform good works to be noticed, because he did not have peace on the inside. People who are not secure with themselves often try to look good, at the same time, they feel the need to criticize others. This was the picture of Judas. He cared what other people thought, because, frankly, he needed their vote.

Make me look good. Accept me! Say that I am OK. Say that what I am doing is OK, even if it is sin. This is how it is with some people. They need to keep perfect order on the outside, because on the inside they feel nothing but chaos. They need the vote of public opinion, and they often do not care, whether or not the public opinion is right.

Only one opinion matters at the end of the day—at the end of your day. Only the opinion of God matters. I see on the inside. You, alone with Me, is all that matters. I am the entrance to heaven. Without My blood on the door of your heart, you cannot be saved, nor enter in to the peace of God. You might think you are safe among the multitude of people who share your beliefs or cause—but one day, you will stand alone before Me.

I was thinking of you, as I am thinking of you now... Take time to reflect inwardly. Take the journey within your heart seriously, before you are faced with selling the Savior for thirty pieces of silver. Judas never did give his life or his money to the poor, did he? Instead, he died a shameful and cowardly death. And his thirty pieces of silver were used to buy a field of death.

In contrast, people who have a pure heart shining from the inside, do not care about people's opinions of how they look on the outside. These precious ones can display their love and worship freely. Mary *loved* Me. She believed I was the Messiah. She believed I was the Son of *Yahuweh*. She listened to Me, and knew in her heart, I could no longer linger on the earth. The thoughts and intentions in her heart, as she anointed Me with oil, were wholesome, and unadulterated.

"Unto the pure all things are pure: but unto them that are defiled and
unbelieving is nothing pure; but even their mind and conscience is
defiled." Titus 1:15

Does this mean she did not have any sin? No—but her heart was so translucent, so transparent, and so genuine, that her spikenard, the precious, costly perfume that she poured out over My head and feet, was only a minute sample of the costly gold she was pouring over Me from her heart. Even though the perfume was worth nearly a years worth of wages, the balm of love, she showered over Me could not be measured.

Mary moved with the essence of a true prophet or priest as she poured the precious oil over My head. In this era, the act of anointing signified selection of someone chosen for a special role or task. Kings were often anointed with oil, by a prophet or priest, as part of their coronation ceremony. Mary, permeated with compassion, fulfilled an unconventional role which set an example for all those who will follow Me— all of whom will demonstrate untethered acts of devotion to Me throughout time.

Rather than measuring out a small amount of oil, Mary breaks the jar and pours the oil out—gushing, life-giving, sacrificing, prayers of incense—over My head. She's completely given herself to the moment. The oil, she may have very well been reserving for her own burial or the burial of a loved one, but instead, she poured it out generously, without thought of her future.

"Give, and it shall be given unto you;
Good measure, pressed down, and shaken together, and running over,
Shall men give into your bosom. For with the same measure that you give,
It shall be measured to you again." Luke 6:38

Can a person out-give God? Whatever you give will return to you, with the same measure as you gave it.

At the local farmer's market in Jerusalem, a good and generous farmer selling his wheat would pour the wheat into the basket, let the buyer shake it, press it down, shake it again, and let the farmer pour his wheat into their basket until it was running over. This same farmer would live in abundance in every aspect of his life. He had given generously to his fellow humankind, therefore would be given back to from his Creator.

Mary did not care *who* was in the room or *how* ridiculous she might have looked to others as she wiped My feet with her hair. The ointment of her pure, unadulterated generosity, which she poured over Me to prepare Me for My burial, comforts Me now. The memory of her fragrant offering and the simplicity of her devotion ministers to Me now.

I am thinking of her now, as I am thinking of you. Those who are pure and beautiful, honorable and true, will have My love, My blood, My life, and My encouragement. You will have My heart when you need it. My heart will be broken for you.

You will have My wounds to heal your broken heart. You will have My broken heart pouring out water and blood for cleansing and nourishment. The aroma of Mary's sacred act, surrounds Me now with the fragrant presence of My Father, who is with Me, as I am with Him. I will remain in this pocket of peace, dwell in this secret space of spices as long as I can.

Before the sun goes down on this day, I will be mocked, beaten, whipped, and stripped. My hands and feet will be nailed to a cross that I must carry up the long winding street of *Via Dolorosa*.

I will be despised, forsaken by men. I will be tortured even more than I can imagine. I will acquaint Myself with grief and for a brief moment will bear the ultimate pain of being separated from My Father. Yet in My suffering, I will bear your diseases, carry your sorrows, your pain, and your deepest anguish.

Even though I am the King of the Universe, I will humble Myself like a lamb led to a slaughter. I will not open My mouth to complain or rebuke the verbal blows of the proud and lofty. I will be cut off from the land of the living. I will be buried with the wicked and with the rich, even though I have done no violence, nor committed any wrongdoing.

Surrounded by the love of many delightful souls like Mary, who will pour out their precious oil over Me for centuries to come, I set My face like a flint toward this certain course — My sacrifice today.

In My nostrils will remain the memory of the fragrant offering poured over Me as Mary wept—an acceptable offering in My sight, one which I will carry with Me to the cross, the hope of the incense of prayers that will rise from the My saints for centuries to come.

As My feet, take one more weary step this morning on My arduous path, I am most comforted by Mary's act of kindness. Her tears have paved the road. Yes. It is worth it. It will be worth it—to walk through this valley of the shadow of death, to become the One name which people must call upon to be saved. I will open the door into eternal salvation for people like Mary, for people like you—for I was thinking of you, as I am thinking of you now...

I pray that in your hour of suffering, and your time of darkness, the harmonious affection of a soul like Mary of Bethany will come alongside you, to soften your heart, to anoint you with prayers, and encourage you to endure your own journey as you carry your cross with Me.

"If you suffer with Me, you shall also reign with Me."
I Timothy 2:12

Now, I must enter the Praetorium. This is the beginning of the end.

Setting...
Entering the Praetorium to be tried before Pilate

Jeremiah 31:31-34; Luke 23; John 18:28-38

As the full moon shone brightly through the windows of Pilate's private chambers, the wife of the Roman Procurator woke up abruptly—covered in a cold sweat.

"That Man," she whispered to herself, "that Man... I could see His face—the one they call the Messiah, Jesus of Nazareth."

"It was a dream," she told herself, but the dream troubled her. She could not go back to sleep after the dream of this Man—this one Man. "I must warn my husband Pilate!" Procula moaned, as she tossed and turned in the early morning...

"I will tell him later today. I do not want to worry him." With that thought, she finally fell back into a troubled sleep, just as Pilate was being awakened for an unofficial meeting with a prisoner. It was just before five a.m. Pilate had been told this prisoner might cause political unrest—this Jesus of Nazareth, who calls himself the Messiah—the Son of God.

The Sanhedrin had pleaded with him the previous night to arrest Me. Pilate had reluctantly given his permission for a regiment of Roman soldiers to cease Me in the Garden.

Pilate thought of his wife sleeping next to him. He could hear her breathing heavily. She had been restless in the night. Pilate groaned softly as he groped for his robe and slippers. It still seemed like nighttime to him. He crept quietly out of the room as to not wake her...

He had hoped the religious leaders would finish the matter among themselves. "Those Jewish leaders, with all of their rules and religious regulations—why are they so bothered by this one Man?" Pilate's thoughts turned and twisted in his head as he prepared himself for the trial. "Surely He has no power over them and if He did have power from a higher source," which Pilate with all his cynicism, could scarcely believe. "So what?! *Why* did they feel so threatened? If His power was coming from

101

their God and they profess they love their God, wouldn't they welcome someone who comes from their God?"

Trying to make sense of it, Pilate continued to reason as he washed his face and put on his governor's robe, "Of what I have seen and heard, this Jesus seems to be a gentle man full of wisdom; in fact, He seems to be somewhat of a sage. If the rumors are true—this country rabbi, who was raised by a carpenter, healed the common folk and fed masses on a hillside with five loaves and two fish."

Pilate obsessively smoothed out the wrinkles in his garment, strapped his sandals to his feet, looked in the mirror one last time, and lingered... "I don't have time for this."

He headed down the stone steps to the gathering place, clearly irritated. He was a busy governor. The Jewish Passover only made his life more hectic with the masses of visitors swarming the streets of Jerusalem.

At the same time Pilate was wishing he could go back to bed, I was nearing the Praetorium with the Roman soldiers and the servants of the high priest. I was bloody, beaten and worn out after being falsely accused, ridiculed, criticized and mocked. I, Jesus, their Messiah, had been treated worse than a common criminal during the three religious trials I had endured, in the palace of the High Priest Caiaphas, which had taken place from just after midnight until now.

First was the questioning before Annas, the former high priest, who was the father-in-law of Caiaphas. Annas passed Me on to Caiaphas to further try Me, after he questioned Me about My disciples and about My teaching.

I had answered him...

"I have spoken openly to the world;
I always taught in synagogues and in the temple,
Where all the Jews come together; and I spoke nothing in secret.
Why do you question me?
Question those who have heard what I spoke to them;
They know what I said."

One of the officers standing nearby struck Me, saying, "Is that the way you answer the high priest?"

I had answered him...

"If I have spoken wrongly, testify of the wrong;
But if I speak rightly, why do you strike me?"

I could have said, "Is this the way you treat your Messiah?" I could have called down a lightning bolt from heaven. But I was not wanting to twist their words to point at them instead of Me. They were already on trial in the courtroom of My Father in heaven.

Then I was bombarded by overblown rhetorical questions by Caiaphas, the high priest; "The one who had advised the Jews that it was expedient for one man to die on behalf of the people." *John 18:13,14*

The high priest said to Me, "I implore you, by the living God, that you tell us whether you are the Christ, the Son of God."

I said to him...

"You have said it yourself; nevertheless I tell you,
Hereafter you will see the Son of Man sitting at the right hand of power,
And coming on the clouds of heaven." Mark 14:62

That is when Caiaphas tore his robes and said to the court, "He has blasphemed! What further need do we have of witnesses? Behold, you have now heard the blasphemy; what do you think?"

They answered, "He deserves death!" *Matthew 26:63-66*

The third trial, still on the palace grounds of Caiaphas, was not a formal meeting of the Sanhedrin. No, it was more like a lynch mob who steals away in the night, too afraid to walk in the light of day. They knew they had no right to execute any man, let alone execute Me. The Jewish leaders had lost the power to determine capital punishment forty years prior to this night. Furthermore, they were forbidden to hold trials at night. But the hypocrites justified their actions by starting the trial after midnight, calling it the 'early morning' instead of the night.

Caiaphas had resolved to execute Me for some time. He now was sitting in the judgment seat over the leaders of Israel and the teachers of the *Torah*. He was determined to push his ideology as far as he could go, and was not known for backing off on points he felt strongly about.

The trials before the Jewish authorities, the religious trials, showed the degree of how much the Jewish leaders hated Me because they carelessly disregarded many of their own laws during My trial—laws such as; no trial was to be held during feast time. Each member of the court was to vote individually to convict or acquit, but I was convicted by acclamation, basically cheering from the members, instead of a vote.

If the death penalty was given by the Roman government, a night must pass before the sentence was carried out; however, only a few hours passed from the conviction to the time I was placed on the cross. The Jews had no authority to execute anyone. No trial was to be held at night, but this trial was held before dawn. The accused was to be given counsel or representation, but I had none. The accused was not to be asked self-incriminating questions, but I was asked if I was the Christ.*

I, Jesus, their Righteous Messiah stood condemned before My chosen ones, who had waited for Me for thousands of years. I remained silent and obedient—obedient unto death. Bound in chains, held in place only by My own decision to become the perfect sacrificial Lamb of God. I endured their unlawful trials for one reason, and one reason only. To pay the ransom for their soul and anyone who would believe on Me.

I was not bound by their courts or judgments. I was not bound by their opinions or laws. I was not bound by the Roman government. Exhausted and alone, after not sleeping for more than twenty-four hours, fettered only by My will to succumb to their misconceptions, I was thinking of you, as I am thinking of you now.

I did not arrive in the manner they were anticipating. Perhaps I am not who you were expecting for a Savior—a humble Messiah, who allowed Himself to be tortured on your behalf. Perhaps you would rather establish your own righteousness, than to join Me in humility and receive My free gift of salvation.

God must be God and show up however He wants or He cannot be God. The priests knew the prophecies in the *Tankah,* those which spoke of Me in Isaiah—the prophecies of a humble king.

I loved all of humanity since I created them. Why would I come to redeem them in such a way which would demand their worship? Any God who is God can exert his omnipotence and power and force people to obey, but I desired to first come in humility and love with the one hope that people would simply love Me back.

I will come again to judge the living and the dead. But now I, the Messiah, Emanuel, the Lion of the tribe of Judah, the Bright and Morning Star, the Prince of Peace—willing to shed My blood to form the new covenant with My beloved people this morning—had come to serve, not to be served.

My blood dripped to the ground as I entered the Praetorium. The pain of my body was minimal compared to the pain in My heart. The suffering that arose from the stark realization that My chosen people of Israel did not recognize their beloved Savior. This was truly the most agonizing pain I felt searing into My heart. My heart beat with longing for them, My first born son, as they continued their condemnation of Me, just as My heart experiences anguish for you, when you do not recognize Me.

Of course, the sin of blasphemy for which the chief priests accused Me of, is atrocious if I was *not* telling the truth — but because I was telling the truth, the sin of delivering the Son of God to die on a cross is the more horrific sin.

The Lamb of God without spot or blemish was prepared to pay the ultimate sacrifice for the sins of Israel and of all people for all time. A God who is God would show up and run the show. The show I was running this day was a reality show of a perfect blood sacrifice for Caiaphas, the Sanhedrin, for Pilate, for Procula, for anyone who would call on My name...

"...not according to the covenant that I made with their Father's
In the day when I took them by the hand
To bring them out of the land of Egypt,
which they broke, even though I was like an Ishi, a husband, to them,
But I will make a new covenant with the house of Israel
And this is the covenant;
I will put my law in their inward parts and write it in their hearts,
And I will be their Adonai and they shall be My people and they shall know
Me, Yahuweh, from the least of them to the greatest of them,
for I, Adonai will forgive their wrongdoings
And remember their sin no more."
Jeremiah 31: 31-34

The New Covenant walked among them, silently carrying their sorrows, at the same time, being despised and rejected. This afternoon, as the sacrifices of the lambs for *Pesach* are taking place, the blood of the Lamb, New Covenant, the *Brit Hadesha*, will enter into death to destroy the power of death. The expressive love of God is not nearly as evident in the resurrection as it is in the death of the Savior. The resurrection exhibits the power of God. The sacrifice unto death, shows the compassion of God,

One who surrenders His power to bear the guilt of those who are powerless.

At the entrance to the Praetoruim, the leaders of Israel accompanying Me stopped abruptly. As recorded, "They who brought Jesus would not themselves enter the portals of the Palace, that they might not be defiled so that they might eat the *Passover*." *John 18:28*

According to Levitical law, the entrance into a heathen house rendered one impure for the day, until the evening. A person who had become Levitically unclean was technically called *Tebhul Yom* (bathed of the day).

Later today, the Passover lambs would be sacrificed and eaten. Yes, the same teachers and leaders of Israel, the ones who followed the Law to the letter, the orthodox of the orthodox, would not defile themselves by entering into the courts of a pagan, but would see fit to let their Messiah, not only enter the courts of a pagan, but be nailed to a cross between two thieves.

Even now, many leaders and teachers of the *Torah* are faced with their Messiah, *Yeshua*, yet even now, they would rather crucify Me than humble themselves and call Me the Messiah of Israel. I know of their zeal. I know of their works, just as I know of your works and know of your zeal. I know when you do no work on the Sabbath. I know how often you wash your hands. I know when you separate milk and meat to the point of having two kitchens so as not to break the rabbinical laws.

I know you keep the appointed Feasts. I know you repeat the blessings. I know how you study the *Torah* all day long, but it is these scriptures that speak of Me. It seems acceptable to you to keep My law, but all day long I stretch out My hands for you to come home to Me—to be completed in Me.

But this day My hands are stretched out to a rebellious house. I came for My own, the lost sheep of the house of Israel, but My own received Me not. In the cleaning and the keeping, the bending and the bowing, they somehow forgot to bow to Me... Jesus, their Messiah, *Emmanuel*.

"You all, as sheep, have gone astray,
each of you going your own way,
And Adonai has laid upon His Messiah the iniquity of all."
Isaiah 53:6

It is for this reason I leave the leaders of the *Torah* outside of Pilate's palace. Led by pagan soldiers, I step into the Praetorium to continue to drink the cup of My Father's will and face the path of judgment. I, in fact, cannot be defiled by anything from the outside, for I am clean by the very nature of My being. I had left the religious leaders outside feeling smug in their outward cleanliness, yet inwardly, they displayed filth and shame—sending their Messiah to bear their sins.

I stood before Pilate, willing to accept their death sentence, for I was sent to die—for I was thinking of you, as I am thinking of you now. I will die for their sins and for yours, so that on the day when your clean white robes are stripped to reveal the unclean truth in your secret heart, you have a Messiah, a Savior, a Lord, who was clean from birth, entered into what was unclean, in order to cleanse My people Israel and the Israel of God—you and anyone who calls on My name.

Procula bolted out of bed, "I *must* warn him. I must warn my husband, Pilate." She frantically called for her maids to dress her. "I must warn him—to have nothing to do with this *Man*." *Matthew 27:19*

GotQuestions.org. "What Trials Did Jesus Face before His Crucifixion?" GotQuestions.org. Got Questions Ministries, 14 June 2017. Web. 08 July 2017.

Setting...
In the Praetorium, the Palace of Pilate

Matthew 7:13-14; Matthew 27:11-14

The Sanhedrin brought Me, the Messiah, the Lamb of God, the Savior and Redeemer of the whole world to be accused before the ruthless governor of the Roman people, Pontius Pilate. Standing here alone,...I was silently praying and thinking of you.

To truly walk with God is to walk alone. One must follow his or her own convictions. A person who follows Me closely will often find themselves ridiculed by others, questioned by those who say they know Me, but really don't, persecuted by those who hate Me, and repressed by those who are simply doing a job.

To walk with God is to tread a long, lonely, narrow path leading to eternal life—a path which often no one understands. No one, except for Me. I am the narrow path.

I am the narrow path this morning, the day of the cross, the day of My sacrifice, the sacrifice of the narrow way—as narrow as My heart which is broken for you—as narrow as My side pierced for you, pouring out blood and water—as narrow as the nails in My hands and in My feet—as narrow as the scarlet thread of redemption prophesied in the curse of the Garden of Eden... "That the seed of a woman would bruise the serpent's head..." *Genesis 3:15*

I am as narrow as a vein of prophecy—the One name being the fulfillment of the three hundred and twenty-eight prophecies in the *Tanakh* concerning the coming Anointed One, the *Mashiah*, the Messiah. I am as narrow as a vein of blood of a suffering servant Messiah who bears the sin of His chosen ones, His people Israel, and the Israel of God. I am as narrow as a Messiah who is cut off, makes Himself a ransom for many... of whom Isaiah had prophesied, the One who would be undesired and rejected by His own people, and the One who would come again and reign as King of Kings, Lord of Lords.

I am as narrow as the seed of Abraham, who through his son Isaac, all families of the earth are blessed—not through the plurality of his descendants, but through One, Me. I am as narrow as the righteous Messiah, coming from the tribe of Judah.

The path is narrow, as narrow as the One standing now before Pilate as the crowd begins to stare and to stir. The chief priests and scribes peer through the gates outside the fence so as not to defile their garments, meanwhile their mouths spew violence and death...

Caiaphas, the High Priest, had said, "It is good if one man died for the people..."

Somewhere in his religiously corrupted mind, he thought he spoke with logic, but his words were ones of murder—to kill someone in order to keep his own gain. He was not thinking of the people. If he was, he would have thought of the thousands of people I had healed, loved, fed, touched, restored, and brought back to life. He would have revisited the prophecies of the Messiah to see if My coming was in line with scripture. He may have even sought solitude—entered into a chamber alone with his God—and asked his Father in heaven if I, *Yeshua,* was the prophesied Messiah.

No. He did none of these things. He had not taken the lonely path or the narrow way. Instead, he argued loudly with Pilate. This morning of the narrow way, surrounded by his tight group of priests, Caiaphas spouted off like a proud, loud-mouthed fool.

Pilate came out, faced the crowd and addressed the Sanhedrin standing outside the gate to his palace. "What charges are you bringing against this man?"

The leaders of the temple answered, "We have found this man subverting our nation. He opposes payment of taxes to Caesar."

I remembered when these same leaders had cornered Me among the people one day, as they attempted to trap Me into saying something against the Roman Government. "Tell us what you think? Is it lawful to pay taxes to Caesar or not?"

I had perceived the question was bait, set up to frame Me, so I answered, *"Why put Me to the test, you hypocrites? Show Me a Roman coin."*

They brought Me a coin of Tiberius. I stated, *"Whose image is embedded in the coin?"*

"Emperor Tiberius Denarius of the Roman Empire," they answered.

Then I said to them, *"Give to Caesar the things that are Caesar's; and give to God the things that are God's."*

Even now, they brought up the tribute money incident in order to continue their accusations, repeating their words in mocking repetition like parrots, squawking sarcastically outside the gate, "This Jesus, claims to be Christ, a king."

I noticed Pilate would not look at Me directly. So often that is how it is with people. They talk about Me in the third person. They speak among themselves about Me while I am here standing in the midst of them.

I stand here now in the midst of them, just as I stand here now in the midst of you, as you are reading the word or studying about Me; conversing or arguing about Me, to discuss the attributes of your Messiah... "When will He come? Who is He? What He will be like? How will you recognize Him when he comes? Will He bring law, justice and order to the world?"

You can discuss and argue points of the Word all day and all night long until you are blue in the face. You continually talk of Me, as if I am not listening, as if I am not in your midst, and yet, here I am in the midst of you. Here I am, Jesus, your Messiah, the Son of God, the Savior of the whole world—you study the scriptures to find Me, yet you don't come to Me—to *know* Me.

You talk of Me, yet you fail to listen—just as My Father said to Job...

"Who are you who darkens counsel by words without knowledge?"

Job 38:2

"Where were you when I laid the foundations of the earth?
Tell Me, if you have understanding.
Who determined its measurements?
Surely you know!
Or who stretched the line upon it?
To what were its foundations fastened?
Or who laid its cornerstone,
When the morning stars sang together,
And all the sons of God shouted for joy?
Or who shut in the sea with doors,

When it burst forth and issued from the womb;
When I made the clouds its garment,
And thick darkness it's swaddling band;
When I fixed My limit for it,
And set bars and doors; When I said,
'This far you may come, but no farther,
And here your proud waves must stop!
Have you commanded the morning since your days began,
And caused the dawn to know its place,
That it might take hold of the ends of the earth,
And the wicked be shaken out of it?
It takes on form like clay under a seal,
And stands out like a garment.
From the wicked their light is withheld,
And the upraised arm is broken.
Have you entered the springs of the sea?
Or have you walked in search of the depths?
Have the gates of death been revealed to you?
Or have you seen the doors of the shadow of death?
Have you comprehended the breadth of the earth?
Tell Me, if you know all this.
Where is the way to the dwelling of light?
And darkness, where is its place,
That you may take it to its territory,
That you may know the paths to its home?
Do you know it, because you were born then,
Or because the number of your days is great?
Have you entered the treasury of snow,
Or have you seen the treasury of hail,
Which I have reserved for the time of trouble,
For the day of battle and war?
By what way is light diffused,
Or the East wind scattered over the earth?
Who has divided a channel for the overflowing water,
Or a path for the thunderbolt,
To cause it to rain on a land where there is no one,
A wilderness in which there is no man;

To satisfy the desolate waste,
And cause to spring forth the growth of tender grass?
Has the rain a father?
Or who has begotten the drops of dew?
From whose womb comes the ice?
And the frost of heaven, who gives it birth?
The waters harden like stone,
And the surface of the deep is frozen.
Can you bind the cluster of the Pleiades,
Or loose the belt of Orion?
Can you bring out Mazzaroth in its season?
Or can you guide the Great Bear with its cubs?
Do you know the ordinances of the heavens?
Can you set their dominion over the earth?
Can you lift up your voice to the clouds,
That an abundance of water may cover you?
Can you send out lightnings, that they may go,
And say to you, 'Here we are!'
Who has put wisdom in the mind?
Or who has given understanding to the heart?
Who can number the clouds by wisdom?
Or who can pour out the bottles of heaven,
When the dust hardens in clumps,
And the clods cling together?
Can you tie the Pleiades or loosen the bonds that hold Orion?
Can you guide the stars season by season?'"
Job 38

Woe to you teachers! Greater will be the condemnation if you teach My sheep out of ignorance and pride. Seek Me while I may be found.
"No longer will anyone need to teach his fellow community member or his
brother—you will know Me, Adonai—from the least to the greatest.
For the new covenant I will make with the house of Israel,
I will put my Torah, my Word, within them and write it on their hearts,
I will be their God, and they will be my people.
I will forgive their wickedness and remember their sins no more."
Hebrews 8:11

Pilate now asks the priests, "What charges do you bring against this man?"

"If he were not a criminal, we would not have handed him over to you," the teachers answered, adamantly.

Pilate answered, "Take him yourselves and judge him by your own law."

"But we do not have the legal power to put anyone to death," the priests answered. They knew that after the ascension of Capunias, the Sanhedrin had lost their ability to try and condemn capital cases. Under the yoke of the Romans, this was the normal policy towards all nations, but the province of Judaea had been spared from this policy up to this point. When Israel lost this right, this signified the removal of the scepter—the tribal staff or national identity of the tribe of Judah.

Jacob, in blessing his sons, prophesied to Judah, "The scepter will not depart from you Judah, nor a lawgiver from beneath your feet until *Shiloh* comes, and the obedience of the nations will be His." *Genesis 49:10*

Ancient rabbis believed that *Shiloh* referred to the Messiah. The scepter had departed from the nation of Israel, because I was now among them. I held the scepter of authority.

Here I was, *Shiloh*, standing before them. The Messiah had come, is come, and will come again. Here I was, the Lion of the tribe of Judah, the one holding the scepter, with the authority over life and death. Here I was, standing in the middle of their two-dimensional conversation, being the multi-dimensional God who actually holds the whole universe, as well as capital punishment in His hands.

"Are you the King of the Jews?" Pilate insisted wishing he could find any reason to vacate this trial.

"Yes, it is as you say," I answered. *"In fact, for this reason I was sent into the world, to testify to the truth. Everyone who is on the side of truth hears My voice."*

"What is truth?" Pilate asked.

Pilate knew deep in his heart that he did not *really* want to know the truth. The truth might be too much for him to shoulder and accept. He might have to leave his position in the Roman government, his livelihood and his reputation.

"Don't you know," Pilate pressed Me, "I have the power to take your life or give you back your life?"

"You have no power except what has been given to you from above," I answered. *John 19:10-11*

The chief priest and scribes now yelled at Me venomously. They sounded like a pit of snakes with slithery tongues hissing relentlessly. "We fear that he will lead the people in a revolution against the Roman government."

I gave no answer to them.

"Don't you hear the testimony they are bringing against you?" Pilate questioned Me. Pilate did not tolerate revolt against the government of any kind. He would stamp out a spark of rebellion immediately if he felt it posed a threat to Rome. Any normal prisoner would not have hesitated to deny this accusation if it were not true. To his astonishment, I continued to give no reply to a single charge.

Pilate retorted again to the leaders of the temple, "You brought Me this man as one who was inciting the people to rebellion. I have examined him in your presence and have found no basis for a charge against this Man."

In the three religious trials, I had been found guilty. In this first trial before the Roman government, Pilate did not see any grounds on which to charge Me. Pilate was desperately trying to find a way to declare Me innocent and thereby release Me, but the Jewish leaders shouted, "If you let this man go, you are no friend of Caesar! Anyone who claims to be a king opposes Caesar!"

This is how it is with people, isn't it? God, incarnate could be standing before them, but instead of worshipping Him, instead of allowing Him to rock their world, they would rather rock His—throw stones at Him and call Him names just as the chief scribes and elders were doing.

Many people would like the path to heaven to be wide, but the path to eternal life is narrow—as narrow as My body—as narrow as an execution stake no more than six inches wide—as narrow as a broken heart pouring out water mixed with blood.

Yes, I was thinking of you as they wickedly cast their insults on Me, as I am thinking of you now... When those who insult Me hurl insults at you accusing you of being a narrow-minded fool if you follow Me, remember, the way is as *narrow* as I am.

"I am the way, the truth and the life—
No one comes to the Father but through Me."

John 14:6

"I and My Father are One."

John 10:30

"Are you the Son of God?" the Scribes and Pharisees asked Me.

"Yes, it is as you say," I answered.

"I am He." I had answered in the Garden.

The way is narrow—as narrow as each obedient step on the streets to Golgatha—as narrow as one choice—a choice between death and life—heaven and hell.

Who do *you* say that I am? Reject Me or Receive Me. I am standing in your midst. I am standing alone. I am knocking on the door of your heart—waiting for your answer.

Pilate and the Sanhedrin thought they had put Me on trial. Pilate thought the outcome would be decided by him, but I was not on trial—they were on trial, just as you are on trial. I am defending and dying for you as I wait for your answer. The one narrow choice you must make—who do *you* say that I am?

Pilate was surprised when his wife motioned for him from the side of the platform. "It must be important if she is interrupting the trial," he thought. He paused to hear what she had to say.

She gazed intently at him, with her face, white as a ghost, as she spoke to him softly in a hoarse whisper, "Have nothing to do with this Man. I suffered much in a dream last night because of Him."

Setting...
Jesus before Pilate at the Praetorium...
Then to Herod's Palace

Luke 23:1-12; John 1:1-14

Pilate's mind was reeling after his wife told him her dream. Romans had a superstition about dreams, especially those which came in the early morning hours. He stepped up his opposition to the Jewish leaders, "I find no basis for a charge against this Man!"

By now, the teachers of the *Torah* could have revoked their charges, they should have revoked their charges, but no, instead they persisted. "He stirs up people all over Judea! He started in Galilee and has come all the way here."

Oh, Galilee! On hearing this, Pilate asked if I was a Galilean. This information made a difference to Pilate since Galilee was under Herod's jurisdiction. Greatly relieved, he summoned the guards to take Me to King Herod, "Send him to Herod Antipas. He is in Herod's jurisdiction." He wiped his forehead and turned his back on Me.

As I staggered forward again, bound and chained, on the way to Herod's palace, I was thinking of Pilate whom we had left behind, at least for now. How he had sighed with relief when he realized he could pass the decision to someone else. This is how it is with human nature. If there is a way to pass the blame, they will pass the blame. If there is a way to avoid answering the question, they will avoid answering the question, the question being—"Who is this Jesus of Nazareth, who calls Himself the Son of God, the Anointed Messiah?"

I was thinking of you, as I am thinking of you now... when you are faced with the one most important decision of your life. "Who do you say that I am?" I am thinking of how you may wrestle with this choice. It is not a one-time choice. It is a day-to-day surrendering to the God who made you and loves you. Sometimes, the choice is not an easy one and when your plans are not in line with My plans, you might hope you can simply send Me away to another jurisdiction.

This is why I have to die for you, for your times of indecision, for God is slow to wrath and full of mercy...

"But you, O Lord, are a God, merciful and gracious,
Slow to anger and abounding in steadfast love and faithfulness."
Psalm 86:15

Just like Pilate who wanted to squirt the issue, just like the Sanhedrin who are hoping to see Me condemned to death, and just like Herod whom we are now approaching—you need mercy. I am the Mercy of God.

As a gentle silent lamb, I was led into the presence of Herod. I will stay quiet now as I continue this journey. I will quietly defend you. I am your defense attorney. I will give everything for your defense. I am defending you even now with each step to the cross—to die for you—in your place, so that when you have completed your trial before the Righteous Judge and are sentenced to die for the crimes of your heart, your sins will be nailed with Me to the cross.

Some say all roads lead to God. All roads do lead to God. God as a perfect, holy, and righteous judge or God as Jesus. The Judge must judge you. You must take the Judgment on yourself, or you must acknowledge Me, that I have taken it on Myself.

There is *no* other way. If there was *another* way, I would not be here, exhausted, bloody, sweaty, thirsty, hungry, beaten, mocked and ridiculed. Now I am in Herod's ring to be beaten and mocked once again— to be heralded as a king without a kingdom and laughed at as a clown.

When Herod saw Me, he was thrilled! He hoped he could see Me perform a miracle. I, on the other hand, saw the fragility of Herod, who talked so tough, yet had no real substance of character or depth of soul. He mocked me, ridiculed Me, as many people do, but I saw right through his empty words, just as I see right through the empty words of others who throughout time will do the same. Underneath shaking skin, on the verge of shattering like glass, I can see their teetering houses built from sand— granules of philosophies, placed carefully, each on top of the other, some truth, some lies, neatly stacked on nothing, with absolutely no foundation in their heart on which to build. Herod's heart exhibited a house of cards with such little stability, I could have blown it away with one sigh.

Herod was secretly terrified of me, but he only shouted louder in order to drown out the still small voice that might have spoken to his heart at some point in his life. Every child has the chance to know Me. Every child, except for the anti-christ, bears an innocence of soul where seeds of faith can be planted and grow. The chief priests and scribes, standing nearby accusing me vehemently, had long sense forgotten their hearts as children,

Herod, who had sacrificed his inner child at the altar of paganism years before, used the priests' rancorous rhetoric as fuel for his puny fire. He pompously ordered an elegant robe to be thrown over my shoulders. As his slaves brought it forth and spread it upon My meek and lowly blood-stained shoulders, Herod laughed hysterically, much like a nervous hyena.

There is the laugh that will sound from heaven, but it is a very different laugh than Herod's nervous cackle.

"Why do the heathen rage, and the people imagine a vain thing?
The kings of the earth set themselves, and the rulers take counsel together,
Against the LORD, and against his anointed, saying,
Let us break their bands asunder, and cast away their cords from us.
He who sits in the heavens shall LAUGH:
The Lord shall have them in derision…
Serve the LORD with fear, and rejoice with trembling.
Kiss the Son, lest he be angry, and ye perish from the way,
When his wrath is kindled but a little.
Blessed are all they that put their trust in him."

Psalm 2

The laugh of God resonates from One who is in control. He who has the last laugh. In contrast, the neurotic laughter of Herod sounded like it emanated from a disconnected electrical wire—waving uncontrollably, spewing out dangerous sparks.

I am the light of the world. Without Me, there is no light. Disconnected wires regurgitating their rhetoric will rule with shock, inconsistency and fear—offer no sustainable true light in which to see the truth. Those who walk in darkness do not even know what they are stumbling over. They are in constant darkness.

Herod was usually an eloquent spokesman, but even he was stumbling over his words as he proceeded to ask Me questions. My indifference clearly bothered him. I could see the sweat gathering on his brow. His eyes began to shift, to and fro, searching the crowd to see if anyone else noticed his *feu de bois*, his burning log, was just about to go out, like a comedian who has lost his crowd after he delivers the first joke.

Why is it that people who have so little to say, talk so very much?

"Are you the Messiah the Jews have been waiting for?" Herod questioned Me. "I hear you can walk on water. Please, give us a show. Or yet, rather turn my water into wine. Oh, pleeeaaassseeee... I hear you touch the lepers—you are not afraid? A king without a kingdom—Do you love a parade? Do fools follow you or have they seen a brighter light? I heard rumors that if the people cease to praise you, the rocks and stones will cry out in praises. If I call the band together—could we have the rocks and stones sing out tonight?"

With one breath I could have knocked him over, just a simple exhale, but what kind of God would I be if I pranced around, showing off? Herod needed a savior, just as much as the next person. If he would only look to Me—cry out for mercy, healing. I would have been his Lord, too.

Herod the Great, Herod of Antipas' father felt threatened when the wise men came from the East, to find Me when I was born. He felt so threatened, in fact, that had successfully at murdered every male child under the age of two, but my earthly father, Joseph, had been warned in a dream. I was whisked away and hidden safely in Egypt. Did Herod of Antipas know I was the boy his father had tried to kill?

He had John the Baptist beheaded. John the Baptist was a prophet, My forerunner, who prepared the way for Me to come. He baptized Me on the brink of My ministry. At My baptism the heavens opened and the Spirit of God descended like a dove. If even for a split second, Herod thought I was the Son of God, he would have been fearful for his *own* head.

But as he continued to mock Me with his nervous laughter, I was not thinking of him any longer, I was thinking of you—when you have mocked Me or laughed at Me or at My servants who come in My name— when the laughter of disbelief shakes nervously inside your soul and you are wondering if you will ever be able to be quiet—simply quiet—when you have ridiculed Me or discounted Me with your friends or your enemies, and now you are done jesting and joking—and you wish you could find a place where your soul is able to rest—simply rest.

It was for you that I could silently bare the ridicule, for I was thinking of you...

I am preparing a place for you to come to when you have nowhere else to run. The place I prepare is My body, the Temple of the living God.

Or perhaps you are the one who has been mocked at, spat upon. Perhaps a loose wire blew sparks at you, singeing you with abuse.

I remained mute as Herod mocked Me and caroused, along with his weak-minded friends. He felt comfortable with his crowd around him. His servants, too, formed a cushion to give him a false sense of comfort. Just like you—in a group you are sometimes able to act stronger, even if you know what you are doing is disturbingly wrong.

I see you in the dark. I see you when you are alone. You may be able to convince the whole world that your sin is all right, but when you are alone with Me in the end of your days, when I turn out the light—if you choose Me, the light of your soul belongs to Me and you will never see darkness. If you *never* open the door to let Me in, you will remain in darkness, singing praises to yourself and those who are like you. You will be cast into the abyss of darkness with those who loved the darkness rather than the light, those who would not come into the light, being afraid that their deeds would be exposed.

Light has no fellowship with darkness. Light, instead, exposes the deeds of darkness. Come into the light now, even now as you hear My voice. I am the light of the world. I can be the light of your world—the light of your soul. Do not run away as the light reveals the secrets of your soul. Instead; confess your sin to Me—in the privacy of your room or your car; in the privacy of your own soul, silently or aloud—confess your sins to Me, Jesus, your Messiah, and I will be faithful to forgive all of your sins. You do not need to tell a priest, although you may if you feel you want to. You do not need to confess to your rabbi, although are free to do so. You need only to confess to Me, your Lord, your Savior...

If only Herod would be quiet long enough to listen to the light. In My light, he would have seen light. If only he allowed the light of truth to pierce to his soul; but alas, the Light stood before him, but he could not comprehend it, just as many cannot comprehend Me—the Light in their darkness, calling to them with all of My heart. I am silent—waiting—defending you before the Father, even as you speak your vacant words like Herod.

When with you very own words you are condemned, I will cry out,
"Father, forgive them, for they know not what they do."

Luke 23:34

Come to Me. Ask Me to forgive you, and I, the silent Savior, will open My mouth and speak forgiveness for you, for only My Father can forgive, in My name.

I had to remain silent in the presence of Herod, so that when you are so loud that your words have boomeranged back to beat you over your own head, My head would be beaten in your place. When the roaring of your own words are drowning you, your makeshift raft of ignorance is crashing over the falls of your own arrogance—you may come to Me and find safety—in Me, for I, the Lamb of God, the righteous Messiah was thinking of you as I stood before Herod, as I am thinking of you now...

You may liberate the actions of many by passing bills and laws, but you will never be able to liberate their souls. You may liberate your own actions and find others to join in, whether these actions are good or not, but you will not be able to find freedom within your heart.

I did not see Herod and his band of loud-mouth fools before Me anymore, I saw prisoners held by the sin of this fallen world—prisoners who served a slimy snake—who fed them with lies—until they knew nothing but death, drowning in cesspools of filth and slime, victims of their own crimes.

Having become completely disconnected to the source of real life, they will persecute the righteous until the day I come again in the clouds with My saints.

I stood before them, being the only hope for eternal life, I, Jesus, the Messiah, the Savior of the whole world, just as I stand before you now. I can see the fragile face behind your mask... Are your jokes starting to crumble? Is the clown make-up beginning to wear off?

Herod could have found rest that day. He could have breathed a sign of relief, yet he was afraid to face the emptiness in his heart, so he only amped up his roar... "Bring a royal robe for our KING!"

Was this necessary? They could have just let me go, but instead, the soldiers violently slung the elegant robes on My weary shoulders. Throughout the rest of today, I will be clothed, I will be stripped, I will be clothed again, then stripped naked—My undergarments ultimately degraded by the soldier's lottery.

Throughout history, I will be stripped. I will be clothed. I will be made into an object of lust. I will be falsely accused. I will be beaten with false accusations. I will be misunderstood. My cross, the means of a pure salvation, will be used, instead, in rituals for darkness and twisted into a symbol of torture by those who hate Me as they persecute those I love.

I will be blasphemed, ridiculed and reasoned away. I will be clarified, corrected, objected to, rejected, cast aside, put on a shelf and placed at the back of the aisle. I will be spat on, laughed at, and cursed. I will be displayed as a woman. I will be accused of being a man who was not divine. I will be hated, mocked, and abused, and yet, I alone, bear the sins of the world.

Before this day is over, I will be nailed to a cross and laid into a grave, but I will I never forsake you, nor have I ever forsaken you. I will sit at the right hand of the Father in Heaven and advocate for you daily. I am your past, present and future defense lawyer. I will be waiting for you, hoping you decide to let Me in, even until your last breath on earth. I am your Savior, and I am still dying in your place daily, meanwhile looking into your face with eyes of love...

Herod, shaking inside—unnerved by My silence—reached a place of his own awkward silence. For a brief moment—a minuscule second, I thought I saw signs of wavering, and hoped he would turn to Me, cry out to Me and call Me Lord—but the silence stripped him, beat him, until he, screaming from the cold of the very empty tomb of his soul, cried out in a shrill voice, "Take him back to Pilate!!"

And that leaves you and Me, alone now. It's between you and Me, Jesus, your righteous Messiah, the Savior of the whole world. Don't wait. Tonight I die on the cross for you. Tomorrow may be too late.

Herod could have stopped to return My gaze, but Herod shook his head instead...

Herod, who had now undone himself, did not want to appear weak. The eyes of his household were upon him. The weight of his decision came down on his neck as a guillotine. No matter what he said from this point, could bring Me back. He has sent Me away. And, without knowing it, each blow to Me, became a blow to his own head. No matter how loud the person is who mocks Me, the names will fall off Me, and return to haunt them instead.

"For whoever is ashamed of Me
And My words in this unfaithful and sinful generation,
the Son of Man will also be ashamed of him

When He comes in the glory of His Father with the holy angels!"
Mark 8:38

Herod held the place of authority in his palace. He held the popular opinion of his people. This was *his* moment. He was in control—or so he thought.

When Herod shook his head, he was not thinking of the ONE who will shake the heavens and the earth one day—the One who will shake His head and say, "Depart from Me, I never knew you." The One who will turn him away from the throne of God and from the eternal paradise.

Herod will be sorrowful then, but I was not thinking of him any longer—I was thinking of you, as I am thinking of you now; that moment, when you seek *Yahuweh* and ask that His face would shine on you, but you realize you need a Savior, someone who would die for your sins.

I had to die for Herod, so that when you are like Herod, mock Me and ridicule My servants who come in My Name, when you demand them to walk on water or raise the dead, when you laugh at them in front a crowd. When the roaring of your own words is causing you to sink on a wild, windy, storm-tossed sea, you can find a silent place to rest in Me. I am right here next to you. Walk on water with Me. Or at least, get in the boat. I will calm the storm.

Are your jokes and shows and chorus lines that chime blasphemies to your Savior starting to crumble? Is your voice beginning to crack? Are you weary in your chaos? Are you tired of good being called evil, and evil being called good?

"Come to Me, all you who labor and are weary
And find rest for your soul." Matthew 11:28

Herod could have found rest that day, if he only would have been brave enough to enter into My silence in order to hear. If he had done this, he might have stole quietly, even in the dark of night, to find Me, like Nicodemus did, but Herod, now shivering with fear, sent Me back to Pilate.

Herod was not thinking—or was he? Were his thoughts truly as evil as his heart, as he uttered his sentence...

"Send him away!"

As Herod witnessed My back turned to him, he could not help but feel the heaviness of the bars coming down and the metal door slamming him into a cold dark room, locking him into the solitary confinement of his decision. He closed his eyes. A stark, vivid, eery memory flashed in his

124

mind, one of John the Baptist's head on a golden platter. Herod put his hand to his own neck.

An uncontrollable chill crept up his spine...

He tried to shake if off.

What will you decide? Decide this day. Don't send Me away—I was thinking of you, as I am thinking of you now...

Setting...
Back at Pilate's

Luke 23:13-25

Pilate exhaled a deep sigh of dismay when he witnessed the band of soldiers leading Me, beaten and worn, back through the gate. He did not lift his eyes to meet Me. At this moment, he did not relish his position as Governor. He felt somewhat annoyed, but saddened that his decision to pass the responsibility of My trial to Herod had backfired.

"Back to square one," he thought. "Why can't these Jewish leaders ease up on this carpenter? He does not seem to be a threat to their position, nor is he a threat to me."

Every eye of the crowd was upon him. The pressure of their stare, was nothing compared to Mine. He could feel Me looking at him, peering into him, through him—piercing through to his very intentions, dividing between soul and spirit, and discerning the thoughts of his heart—with such precision, as one who could divide bone from marrow; for after all, I am the Word of God. The Word made into flesh, the living Torah. The Truth of the Word burned through Me, a laser beam of light, seared through My eyes. *Hebrews 4:12: John 1:14*

The Word, who was with God and was God, who was born, not of blood, nor of the will of the flesh, nor by the will of man, but born of God, stood before Pilate, full of grace and truth. "The law was given by Moses, but grace and truth came through Me, the Messiah." *John 1:17*

Pilate thought that he stood as judge in the judgment seat, but I was in the position of judge, but I came not to judge him, but to save him. With my compelling, compassionate eyes, I hoped to persuade him *not* to listen to public opinion nor to the High Council of Caiaphas. I hoped beyond hope that he might pay attention to the beat of his own heart; or if not that, at least give serious heed to his wife's dream.

Pilate remembered the rumors floating around of John the Baptist. He had heard, that when John baptized this Jesus of Nazareth, he cried out,

"This is He, whom I told you about! He who was coming after me, but is preferred before me!" *John 1:15*

Pilate wondered why Herod decided to behead this man. What could he have done wrong? What could this man, Jesus, standing before me now have done wrong? They both seemed like religious zealots. Is that a bad thing? Jesus fed people and healed them. Neither one was violent, or rude, nor had they stolen anything or caused a riot.

The crowd did not notice Pilate's jaw tighten and his facial muscles flinch, while he reflected on the beheading of John the Baptist, but I noticed. He certainly did not want to share in the responsibility of putting innocent men to death. In fact, he did not even desire responsibility *per se*. No, it was political power that he enjoyed, for he had a weak spine after all. Many politicians will follow suit over many generations. A good one is rare.

Now that I stood before him, looking more like a tortured criminal than the Son of God, Pilate's political mind began to kick into place, rather than a mind of reason. "Herod sent him away. Maybe Herod knows something I don't know. He, nor I, are well versed in the Jewish religion. If the leaders of the *Torah* are shouting to condemn this man, then perhaps Herod is right?! What's one more criminal put to death?"

"Herod and I will become friends after this," Pilate thought. "We can commiserate together and perhaps we will be even more powerful. Politicians feed off each other when their agendas line up. He hadn't thought of being friends with Herod before. In fact, they were not close at all, and rarely, if ever did they agree. Now, faced with a common factor of guilt, he felt he might feel more comfortable in a group. Even a group of two.

"Get on with it!" The chief Scribes bellowed outside the gate! "He has committed blasphemy! He says he is the Son of God!"

With the clamour of the priests, Pilate snapped out of his dream state, where he was bolstering his career bubble with Herod's liaison. He deliberated once again, "I have examined Him and find no basis for your charge against Him! Neither has Herod found any fault in him. He sent Him back to me because he has done nothing to deserve death; therefore, I will punish Him and release Him." *Luke 23:4*

The shouting of the crowd grew very loud at this time. They accompanied the priests now, as they continued to ooze their grumbling to irritate the festering sore they had created. The cancerous rumbling now planted in the stomach of the hungry mob would not stop until they were satisfied by devouring something or someone that day. Crowds are never satisfied because they are not a being, but a collective. A collective does not have a conscience. Mobs today and throughout time cannot be trusted.

"Why so early in the morning?" Pilate moaned, "Why... Why must we rush these matters? Why today on Passover?"

He looked upon his prisoner. Not into My eyes, no, but onto My frail-looking, human body, bleeding and trembling, starving and sleep deprived, contrasted with the angry mob. I resembled a small white lamb surrounded by a hungry pack wolves.

Pilate felt the pressure of the Sanhedrin and the Council. He felt the pressure of the venomous crowd. He felt he was in a boxing match with fate, and he knew he was beginning to be backed into the ropes. He was unwilling to step out of the ring for fear he would appear soft and not at all like the ruthless Roman governor of Judea, which was of course, his repuation.

"Look at Me," I pleaded with My eyes. "Look into My eyes." I knew Pilate when he was a boy; so petite, so frail. He was not cut out to be a soldier. He got pushed around by the bigger boys. Bullied even. But he was extremely smart and he knew he could succeed in politics if he used his mouth wisely. The scene set before him this morning; however, did not seem like a political matter.

"*Why* is this decision falling on me? Just because the Jews cannot punish their own?" he thought to himself again. "This is madness."

As he was thinking these thoughts, I was thinking of him, as I was thinking of you. Often the structure of a system or organization will box you into a corner just as Pilate felt boxed into a corner now. When you are up against the ropes, forced to make a life-changing decision based on your own integrity, or giving in to a loud group of bullies like Pilate, I hope you will look to Me. I hope you will see the truth standing before you, outside the religious or governmental system, and I hope you will stand up for yourself, for Me, and chose truth.

I was thinking of you, as I am thinking of you now. I know Pilate will not make the right decision, but you can. You can see beyond the rhetoric, beyond the chaos of this world. Choose Me. Choose the narrow path of righteousness which leads to eternal life.

Pilate was frustrated this morning by the system and hierarchy of the church and state. Yes, he was fully aware that the Jewish leaders could not condemn Me to death by execution at this time, unless they stoned Me. *Jus gladii*, supreme jurisdiction, belonged only to Rome. The priests had a ultimate agenda. They were determined to push for a formal decision by the Romans, in order to trace the final decision in a clear line of command. In a nutshell, so they could pass the blood from their hands to the Romans.

As I have stated, the Jewish leaders stayed outside of the judgment hall, so they would not be defiled. I knew their reasoning and to them it made such sense. They knew that contact with a Gentile meant defilement as the "heathens" were unclean, so they rationalized even to the point of ridiculousness.To maintain cleanliness as the Passover approached, the religious leaders avoided contact with Gentiles, yet were pleased to send their Messiah into the unclean arena.

I had said to them...

"Woe unto you, Scribes and Pharisees, hypocrites!
For you are like whitewashed sepulchers,
Which indeed appear beautiful outwardly,
But are within full of dead men's bones,
And of all uncleanness."

Matthew 23:27

Out of the abundance of the heart, the mouth speaks. The hypocrisy of the religious leaders who accused Me of blasphemy, is not unlike many hypocritical religious leaders who will lead the organized church throughout centuries. Wolves in sheeps clothing, or wolves in shepherd's clothing—even worse.

Tradition will rule. Greed will reign. Many true believers and followers of Me, Jesus, the Messiah, the Savior of the whole world, will be beaten, scourged, mocked, burned at the stake, and even hung on a cross. Over and over, I will be set on the judgment seat and condemned to death, through each precious martyr who will suffer with Me and die with Me. They who suffer with Me will reign with Me, but those who lie and make a lie—who rule the false church—will be forever shut out of My kingdom.

My kingdom is built with living stones. Hearts of flesh who are willing to identify with Me in My death and thus live with Me forever. The true church throughout history will be invisible to most for... "I look on the heart of mankind, not on the outside." *I Samuel 16:7*

I see your heart today, for I was thinking of you just, as I am thinking of you now at the trial. The trial of your faith is so very precious and valuable to Me. As you follow Me along an often solitary path, at times no one will understand, just as no one in the crowd understands Me today, not *one* of them understood—that the One standing before them is the Way, the Truth, and the Life, the Messiah and Savior of the whole world.

What hypocrisy—to be preoccupied with a meaningless tradition while attempting to execute the Son of the living God! The religious leaders maintained a fastidious commitment to their religion while seeking to kill the source of their religion, their very own awaited Messiah. They misunderstood Me today, and will misunderstand Me for thousands of years, until I come again, and they will see Me, and know that it is I whom they have pierced. *Zechariah 12:10; Revelation 1:7*

"Wait! Hold on! Perhaps there is a way out of this!" Pilate suddenly remembered one of their Roman customs. He signed a great sign of relief. Today, on Passover, Pilate could release one prisoner who was sentenced to die.

"Surely, they will call for the release of this man, Jesus of Nazareth, whom I can find no fault with," he encouraged himself. "This will be my answer. I will flog him and let him go."

But as he was summing up his own conclusion which would exonerate him from this filthy plot—the accusations from the Sanhedrins escalated along with the angry shouts from the crowd.

I could barely hear him above the noise of the crowd when Pilate said, "So you are a king?"

I responded, "You say I am a king. Actually, I was born and came into the world to testify to the truth. All who love the truth recognize that what I say is true."

"What is truth?" Pilate asked.

Then he went out again to the people and told them, "He is not guilty of any crime. You have a custom of asking me to release one prisoner each year at Passover. Would you like me to release this 'King of the Jews'?" *John 18:37-39*

For a split second there was silence and the space and time continuum seemed to stop. You could have heard a pin drop in the huge stadium...

Then one single voice in the crowd shrieked, "Release to us, Barabbas!" That one voice pierced My ear. I knew the person from whom that voice originated, just as I know your voice. I had created the person, knit him together in secret, in his mother's womb. I had given him his unique voice, yet I had also given him a choice, as I have given to each person—as I have given to you. This one voice was loud enough to incite the crowd like a spark from one match carelessly thrown to the ground that ignites a ferocious forest fire. As it is with a wild fire, the rest of the crowd savagely joined in, with a violent chant that would change the course of all human history, "Release to us Barabbas! Release to us Barabbas!"

My treasured followers were completely scattered by now. The scene exploded into a mob scene. Mobs are unpredictable, but I was not afraid. I knew the rant of this ugly crowd would only get louder. My disciples cowered in fear. They could not have imagined their leader being treated in this manner.

I do not blame them for their fear. I do not blame them for fleeing. I was thinking of them, just as I am thinking of you now—when you are in a crowd of people who mock My existence, who would ridicule you if you dare say that you are a follower of Me. I know there will be times when you shrink back with fear. I am praying for you. I pray that you will overcome the fear with faith, because greater am I, who are in you, than the shouts of a noisy crowd.

I wanted to hush each person in the crowd. I wanted to silence their demands for their own sake. Some of them had been healed by Me. Some had been raised to life and delivered from evil spirits, but mobs can be hideous and one revolting voice can insight a riot, while softer voices can be muffled under the weight of the others.

Dark hearts find comfort in crowds. A pure heart can stand alone, just as Stephen, My disciple, will stand alone when he becomes the first martyr—stoned to death by those who claimed to be My own. Surely those stoning him will be mesmerized and ashamed when they behold his face shining towards My Father in heaven as the stones are being hurled at him.

"Stephen, full of the Holy Spirit, will look up to heaven
And see the glory of God,
And Me, Jesus, standing at the right hand of God."

Acts 7:5

My kingdom is not of this world. Throughout many years of history after My death and resurrection, there will be martyrs such as Stephen, who will lay down their lives to build the foundation of the church, the true living church. Where two or three are gathered in My name I am present among them. My living church will be built on the blood of the martyrs.

I already knew what Stephen would say to the evil hearts of the Sanhedrin who are condemning Me to death now. Stephen will say...

"Look, I see heaven open
And the Son of Man standing at the right hand of God."

Acts 7:55

And I already knew what the leaders would do...

"At this the teachers and leaders of the torah covered their ears
and, yelling at the top of their voices, they all rushed at him, dragged him
out of the city and began to stone him. While they were stoning him,
Stephen prayed, 'Lord Jesus, receive my spirit.'
Then he fell on his knees and cried out,
'Lord, do not hold this sin against them.'
When he had said this, he fell asleep."

Acts 7:58-60

Of course he will not fall asleep. He will come to Me. His martyrdom, as I have predicted it, fills me with love for him now and gives Me courage to continue today on the path of suffering. For all of those who, like Stephen, will give their lives for Me, also give Me courage to press on, as I give them courage by completing My mission.

I will die for this mob and for the one voice who incited the riot so that if ever you have incited a riot or been part of a mob which has caused an innocent to die, an innocent will die in your place, Me. When the mob scene is over and you are left alone with blood stained hands, all you need to do is ask for forgiveness, turn from your wicked way and you will be forgiven—for I was thinking of you, as I am thinking of you now.

Or if you are the one who has been trampled by a mob... you have a Lord who has suffered the same. I love all of *My own.* I give My life for the whole world, but those who come to Me, I will make a covenant with My blood—dearly beloved—and sealed with Me forever.

I was momentarily lost in My thoughts of these precious souls, all who would love Me throughout thousands of years, when suddenly, rudely, I was forced to return to the current scene.

Pilate proceeded to invoke the crowd again to let Me go, "Neither I nor Herod have found anything done by this Man that is worthy of death. I will therefore chastise him and release Him."

Even though the chastisement meant thirty-nine lashes of the most excoriating pain which could be inflicted on a human being, the mob responded with a tidal wave of disappointment. They booed even louder with their angry voices, tongues waving in the air as a whip being tossed haphazardly, like confetti, "Away with this man! RELEASE UNTO US Barabbas! BARABBAS! BARABBAS!"

I could hear them chant. "Release unto us, Barabbas!"

Barabbas was just a man, a common criminal. I knew what he had done. He was not worse than any man; in fact, those who say they are righteous but have hearts darkened by evil are just as bad as the Barabbases of the world. Some are even worse. Barabbas was, of course, happy and relieved to be chosen by the crowd. I knew he would be and I was also happy for him. I was thinking of him, just as I was thinking of you, just as I am thinking of you now...

When you are in a tough predicament, perhaps by your own doing, I will release you. Barabbas' name meant "Son of the father," and truly, he is a son, to the same degree as anyone. If Barabbas had called out to Me for forgiveness, he would have had it, just as you will receive my forgiveness when you have committed a common crime or a crime of the heart, if only you call upon My name. I am the scapegoat for Barabbas today, just as I will be your scapegoat.

My mind is reeling now. The noise of the crowd is deafening. There is a smell of sulphur in the air emitting from the sins of angry men and women—very unlike the sweet smell of incense radiating from the prayers of humble servants like Mary.

With one word from My mouth, I could slaughter my captors, or cause them to be ousted by a giant wind. I could burn them with fire. I could cause an earthquake to open up the ground and swallow them, but I was thinking of them. They needed a Savior and I was, I am, the only one who could cover their sins.

I was thinking of you, if you are rushed along with an angry mob, perhaps to make the wrong decision or chose the wrong savior. When you realize what you have done and you need atonement for your sins, you have Me, condemned to die for you. When the crowd has dispersed and you are alone in your closet, scared and frail, I will break My body for you and cover you with My blood. I pray you will find a place of silence away from the crowd. Step away from an angry mob before you are swept out to sea by the current tide of public opinion...

I was thinking of you as I am thinking of you now...

Setting...
Pilate's Place of Judgment—Gabbath

Matthew 27:19-28

Now Pilate and his cohorts brought Me to the place of Judgment known as Gabbath. It was the 6th hour on the Day of Preparation. This would be the final setting before the decision to condemn Me to death.

Herod and Pilate became friends today. Isn't it sad how enemies become friends when united against God? Perhaps it is their weaknesses that cause men and women gather in groups when criticizing Me. Perhaps insecurities drive them together.

A person is less apt to speak against God on a lonely desert plain in the middle of the night. The stars, alone, shine so brightly they swallow up cynicism with heavenly praises. One can find strength when one is alone in nature—a symphony the universe outshines the stuttering and stammering of sarcasm and group think.

I had walked alone when I was tested in the desert, I had to walk alone this day, as the crowd shouted for the release of Barabbas. The crowd somehow felt superior when faced with a murderer or criminal. Perhaps it is easier to hide behind the weak than to face the Messiah Jesus, who calls Himself, God.

When one is face to face with God, for I am the face of God, the invidious voices and doubts of one's own conscience are called into account in the omnipotent presence of God. Public opinion is drowned out simply by the fact that *I am He*.

Perhaps in your guilt, you do not know what to say and the words of your own justification are caught in your throat. It is then you need a Savior who takes your iniquity—completely, and absolutely, without uttering a word of deceit. In fact, no deceit was found in My mouth.

This is why I remain silent today, for I was thinking of you... The day when the accuser of the brethren incriminates you, brings up your guilt, your misdeeds, your wrongdoings and beats you over the head with your sin. It is then you need a Savior who *knew* who He *was* and who He *is*, a Savior who needs no defense. When you have no defense, I am your defense. When the accusers of your soul are shouting, "Crucify him! Crucify her! He deserves to die! She deserves to suffer for what she did." I am your defense. I die in your place. Your sins are remembered no more. I put them as far as the East is from the West.

Perhaps you are innocent, but your accusers do not believe you. It is then you need a Savior who was falsely accused. I have gone before you —paved a path for you in humility and meekness, all the way to heaven.

The roar of the crowd around Me continued, "Crucify Him! Crucify Him!"

When Pilate was about to completely buckle under the crowd's pressure, he remembered his wife's dream. He remembered her pale, torn face looking up at him with her sweet, trusting eyes when she whispered in her eerie tone, "Have nothing to do with this man. I suffered much in a dream last night because of Him."

Pilate loved his wife. He respected her, but what is a dream? What is truth? Could a warning in a dream be counted on? Can a dream prove to be a valid reason to ignore a screaming frenzied mass? Of course it can. But people over the centuries to come will often not give a second thought to a woman's dream or anyone's dream for that matter, even though many dreams are given to people for warnings. If Pilate told the crowd he could not crucify Me because of his wife's dream, they might pick up stones and throw them at him instead. A frightening thought, but perhaps this could have saved his soul.

"Fear not them which kill the body, but are not able to kill the soul:
But rather fear Him which is able to destroy both soul and body in hell."
Matthew 10:28

Pilate could not forget the image of his wife as she gripped her stomach nervously while she spoke, as if the knots in her stomach would become knots around his throat...

Sweat poured down his brow. "The crowd is shouting much too loud," he screamed inside of his head, "won't someone stop the shouting! I must get ahold of myself. I have a reputation to uphold," he frantically debated with himself, "I will have work it out with my wife later." One more chance, One more chance. Pilate decided as he unclenched his hands around his own throat, "I will give the crowd *one* more chance to relent."

Pilate faced the maddening crowd, much like facing a ravenous beast in a jungle and emphasized for the *third* time, "I find no fault in this man!"

"Release unto us Barabbas!" "Release unto us Barabbas!"

"What shall I do with this man Jesus?" Pilate retorted.

"Crucify him!"

"Crucify him!"

"What has he done?" Pilate implored the mob at the top of his lungs now, but the deafening roar of the crowd drowned out his voice.

"Crucify him!" "Crucify him!"

As I silently listened to their protests, I thought about each one of them. I knew each person intimately. I knew the number of hairs on each of their heads. I had woven each of them together in their mother's womb. In the darkness, I had formed each body, each brain, every organ, giving each of them their specific DNA. My thoughts toward each of them were more than the grains of sand of the sea. I knew when they arose in the morning. I knew when they sat down. I knew each word on their tongue, just as I know your words, your thoughts, just as I know your going out and coming in. I was thinking of them, just as I am thinking of you now...

Destiny was in My Hands. I was not afraid.

Pilate, however, was quite terrified when he clearly could see that even after all of his pleading, he had failed. Surely, his reasoning was sound. But how can one reason with the unreasonable?

Utterly defeated, a dark cloud came over him. He felt like a nervous rabbit, caught in a trap, surrounded by hungry coyotes. He stared, but not at Me, more like through Me. Hoping there was a way out. He wondered how I had gotten Myself into this predicament. He shook his head with pity.

I did not pity myself. I did, however, pity him. He was caught in the middle of My people Israel whom I came to save—the sons and daughter who descended from Abraham, Isaac, and Jacob. I was their long awaited Messiah. I had come to them, but they did not receive Me. They did not recognize Me—their much longed-for King, Deliverer, *Mashiach*, who was the One appointed by *Yahuweh*, who descended from the *Davidic* line to rule the united tribes of Israel. I stood before them now, just as I had stood before them in the temple on the Feast of *Sukkot*.

On the last day of the seven day feast, I proclaimed publicly...

"If anyone is thirsty, let him or her come to me and drink.
Whoever believes in Me, as the scripture has said,
Streams of living water will flow from within him."
John 7:37-38

I knew full well the significance of what I was saying. The Jewish leaders of the temple knew what I meant, as well, but they only added it to their list of blasphemous statements which they accused Me of making.

During *Sukkot,* the Feast of Tabernacles, My people Israel carried torches around the temple, illuminating bright candelabrum along the walls of the temple to demonstrate the coming Messiah, who would be a light to the Gentiles as well. The priest would draw water from the pool of Siloam and carry it into the temple where it was poured into a silver basin beside the altar. The priest would call upon *Yahuweh* to provide heavenly water in the form of rain. Many people looked forward to the future, to the pouring out of the Holy Spirit, the latter harvest, as was spoken by the prophet Joel.

When I proclaimed that *I* was the living water, I was proclaiming to be the source of the water, the *Mayim Hayim*, Living Water coming straight from heaven. When I, then exclaimed,

"I am the light of the world. Whoever follows Me will never walk in
darkness, but will have the light of life." John 8:12

The people in the temple understood that I was claiming to be *the* Messiah, the light to both Jews and Gentiles. Sadly, they were too blind to see the light who stood before them.

No. I did not pity Myself. I knew what I must do. I did pity Pilate, however, for even though he would make his decision with a sorrowful heart, not one of anger, malice or greed—he will still be swayed by public opinion which will be his ultimate downfall. I, also, had pity for My people Israel, for O, how they would suffer after this night.

"O Jerusalem, Jerusalem, the city that kills the prophets
And stones God's anointed ones.
How often I have longed to gather your children together
As a hen gathers her chicks,
How often I would have gathered them under My wings."
Luke 13:34

I knew a time was coming soon, after they rejected their Messiah, that Jerusalem would be under siege and taken from them for nearly two thousand years. For this long period of time, they will be scattered throughout the earth.

When Israel becomes a nation again, and they inhabit Jerusalem, the times of the Gentiles will be fulfilled. *Luke 21:24* The Gentile church age will rise up and be a predominate presence on the earth until 1967. After a six day war, when the Jews capture Jerusalem once again, I will pour out my spirit on Jew and Gentile and they will become one new man. *Ephesians 2:14-16* For I am indeed the Light to the world, both Jew and Gentile.

As the mounting doom gathered against Me, I remembered the previous week, when I rode into Jerusalem on a donkey, exalted as a King. The shouts coming from the crowds at this procession were shouts of joy, gladness, praise and exaltation. Many people who were *now* shrieking, "Crucify him!" were *then* shouting with glee, "Long live the King! God has given us a King! Let heaven rejoice! Glory to God in the highest. Hallelujah!"

The euphoria of the adoring crowd did not effect Me that day, neither does the clamor of this belligerent crowd effect Me now. I am not swayed by public opinion. I do only what I see the Father doing. I live only to please My Father in Heaven. I am without blemish, perfect in every way. I cast no stones against the crowds. Whether the public is for Me or against Me is of no consequence to Me. The consequence remains solely with each person's decision in his or her own heart.

I remain the same—yesterday, today and forever. I was thinking of them, as I was thinking of you—just as I am thinking of you now... When the waves of the masses ebb and flow and you are drifting alone on your own raft, troubled, being tossed to and fro on the waves of indecision, you can call upon Me. I will calm the storm. I will walk on the water and reach out My hand to you and say...

"Take courage! I am. Don't be afraid." Matthew 14:27

You will notice there are wounds in my wrists and the wounds will make you whole. I was thinking of you, as the crowds were shouting both with glee or with anger. I could hear *your* cry amidst the crowd and I set my face like a flint to accomplish the task of *your* salvation. I could also hear your shouts, some of when you are praising Me for what I have done and other times when you are cursing Me for what I have not done, that you think would have been better for you. I know this will be a constant struggle for many, but...

"My Ways are not your ways,
And My thoughts are not your thoughts.
My Ways are higher than your ways,
My thoughts, higher than your thoughts.
For as the heavens are higher than the earth,
So are My ways higher than your ways,
And my thoughts than your thoughts.
For as the rain comes down, and the snow from heaven,
And returns not but waters the earth, and makes it bring forth and bud,
That it may give seed to the sower, and bread to the eater:
So shall My word be that goes forth out of My mouth:
It shall not return unto Me void, but it shall accomplish that which I please,
And it shall prosper in the thing whereto I sent it."

Isaiah 55:8-11

There will be things that happen in your life you do not understand. My beloved, just as no one understands My journey today, no one understood the meaning of My joyous procession to the Mount of Olives. The crowds, on that glorious day, who spread their robes along the road ahead of Me expected a king who would rule the earth, instead of a King who would be crucified to make a way into heaven, for His Kingdom is not of this earth.

During the procession, the Pharisees had murmured among the crowd. They commanded Me, "Sir, rebuke your followers for saying things like that!"

But I replied...

"Even if the crowd keeps quiet,
The rocks and stones along the road will burst into Hosannas."

Luke 19:40

I could not share in the joy that day which many of you now celebrate as Palm Sunday, for I knew what would happen to Jerusalem and the temple after My death. I knew what would happen to My people for thousands of years as they were driven from Jerusalem.

As we came closer to Jerusalem, I began to cry in My Spirit...

"Eternal peace was within your reach and you turned it down!
It is now too late.

The enemies will pile up earth against your walls,
Encircle you, close in on you, crush you to the ground.
Your children will suffer with you.
There will not be one stone left upon another in the temple, as you have
rejected the new Temple standing before you."

Luke 19:42-44

Even though most of My people will forsake Me, all of My first disciples and followers are Jewish and they will become the foundation of My church. The leaders of My temple, who were hard of heart, would not share in this foundation. Often this is how it is with organized religion. Many followers are pure in heart, whereas power in leadership often turns good people into evil ones. This is why I had to curse the fig tree the next day after the procession. The fig tree represented the hearts of My people Israel who were in charge of the temple in Jerusalem. My temple was to be a place of prayer, but they had made it a den of thieves. It had to crumble because they had rejected the plan of *Yahuweh*.

Pity, isn't it—when one cannot recognize God because of a hard heart?

Pilate shook his head now, not at Me, but at the crowd. As the weight of the masses pressed him down, he sorrowfully made his final decision. He then took water and symbolically washed his hands while the crowd stared at him. He said, "I am innocent of the blood of this just man." Even though he stated it with resolve, as if he could absolve his own guilt; even though he washed his hands—he remained guilty as he gave me over to their wishes, "See to it."

You might have thought the crowd would feel a hint of shame or a hush of remorse. Perhaps one or two might have felt the chilly reverberation of the unjust sentence that had just been uttered; but no, the noise only escalated and their commitment to see Me crucified more obstinate. They now, in great ignorance, pleaded loudly..."Let his blood be on us and on our children."

I cast My head to the ground. I remembered the night before when I sweat drops of blood as I whispered, "Not My will, but Yours, be done."

My Father knew the course this day would take. It was prophesied many years ago by the prophets. The Jewish leaders knew of these prophecies, they just did not accept the way in which they were fulfilled. Years later, when they inhabit Jerusalem again, most of them will still be

143

looking for another *Mashiach*, instead of Me, Jesus, *Yeshua*, their righteous Messiah. To their surprise, I will come in the clouds to stand on the Mount of Olives as the risen and reigning King of the universe. They will weep, as one who has lost an only son, when they gaze upon Me—He whom they pierced.

The verdict of death is progressing so quickly now. I guess this is how it is with bad decisions. Move them along quickly, without prolonging the tragedy. If one takes too much time to think, one might actually change one's mind. Ludicrous decisions are like a mudslide. Usually it is not one decision that causes the disaster, but many small decisions put together, finally becoming a sum of wrong choices, an unstable foundation. Many small stones of truth, taken out of the cliffside, a stone tossed aside here, another there, until there is nothing left but slippery sand, silt, mud. All it takes to topple, is a little rain.

Therefore whosoever hears these sayings of Mine,
And does them, I will liken him unto a wise man,
Which built his house upon a rock:
And the rain descended, and the floods came, and the winds blew,
And beat upon that house; and it fell not:
For it was founded upon a rock.
And every one that hears these sayings of Mine, and does them not,
Shall be likened unto a foolish man, which built his house upon the sand:
And the rain descended, and the floods came, and the winds blew,
And beat upon that house;
And it fell: and great was the fall of it. Matthew 7:24-27

This was how it was with Judas. At each crossroads, he could have softened his heart and followed in the correct path I must take, just as Pharaoh could have softened his heart and saved his first born son by setting the children of Israel free in Egypt. Each one might have delivered himself from his very own hour of darkness.

My hour of darkness was fast approaching, it was upon Me now—the darkness of human hearts who would rather crucify their Messiah than worship Him. Sinful hearts who would rather set a murderer free than release the blameless One, completely free from sin.

The thick, heavy veil of the temple, which separates the Holy of Holies from the people, I will tear in half in the hour of My death. The ripping of this veil, will open a door, so that anyone who calls on My name can enter into intimate fellowship with *Yahuweh*. Yet, this same veil, will be a symbol of the veil which will remain over the eyes of My people Israel for nearly two thousand years.

As the shouts began, "Let His blood be on *our* hands and upon *our children's* hands," I looked down at My hands—the Hands that hold the universe in a span. My hands would be covered in blood in a few hours as I am ruthlessly nailed to an execution stake by their hands. And yet, the irony of guilt upon one's hands will be absorbed by the wounds in My hands. The blood which will pour from My hands will be available to them for redemption—freedom from guilt.

I shuddered with a shudder that rocked the universe as the shouts continued. A tidal wave of blood, of doom, and of death ripped the atmosphere of time and space—of order and of goodness. I saw past, present, and future. I knew their children—their children's children—their generations for time and times and time to come. I thought of how they would be scattered over the earth for almost two thousand years. A chill now pierced my spine. A different chill than that of Herod's impending doom. This chill was for the persecution My people would suffer.

I could have stopped the audacious scene. I could have torn the troposphere with a bolt of lighting. I could have split the ground in two. I could have disappeared, Poof! But no, I persisted to remain upright in My mangled messy blood stained robe, for I was thinking of you...

The matter would be blood now. Sin requires a blood sacrifice. Blood must be shed because of arrogance. Blood must be shed because of ignorance.

I persevered to go through with this death in order to shed My Blood to cover you, for I was thinking of you, as I am thinking of you now... When you have sinned and fallen short of the glory of God—when you have caused a little one to stumble and the blood is still on your hands, you can wash your hands and your heart in My blood.

Pilate frantically washed his hands, but he did not feel clean. From this day on, he would now have nightmares, waking up with blood stained hands, unable to scour them spotless again.

Oh, if he would have listened to the warning in his wife's dream, but how often do people listen? How often do they act? The blood on the hands of the crowd, the blood they asked for, will create an outpouring of bloodshed for generations to come. Somehow, the washing of their hands never seemed to cleanse the stain, not after today. Even to this day, My religious people of Israel wash their hands. They wash. They wash. But remain unclean.

Only the blood of Jesus, the righteous Messiah, can wash away sin.

"Though your sins be as scarlet, they will be white as snow."

Isaiah 1:18

There will be judgment on the world. It must be so. How could someone serve an unrighteous God? If *Yahuweh* lets people get away with evil doings, what kind of trust can you put in Him?

But just as God is judge, He is also Jesus. As My Father judges, I, His Son, have stretched out My hands and will allow them to be pierced— so that the blood will be on My hands instead. I willingly take the judgment upon Myself, for them— and for you.

And the blood will keep pouring, to their children, to their children's children and to you throughout every generation, until I return as King—for I was thinking of their children, just as I was thinking of you, as I am thinking of you now. When your hands are soiled with sin, and never feel quite clean, put your hands in mine. I will wash them as white as snow. I, the living *Torah*, was thinking of you and I am thinking of you now.

Setting...
The Scourging

Matthew 27:26; John 17

On the side of the platform of the Praetorium, I could see Barabbas being released. How relieved he was—a murderer, a dead man walking to his certain execution, now being freed by the incantations of the anxious crowds pleading before Pilate. Did he know that I was the One who was actually releasing him? How could he have known? I did not look much like a King, yet I was happy for his exaltation, because I was thinking of him.

My blood had already set one prisoner free. Even before I finished My work on the cross, I was setting the captives free. Throughout time, I will set many prisoners free. Some, like Barabbas, will never totally understand that it is I who have done it. You see...

"My Father causes his sun to rise on the evil and the good,
And sends rain on the righteous and the unrighteous." Matthew 5:45

I will continually pour out grace and mercy upon My people, My children of the Earth. Only some, very few, will turn around and thank Me. Out of the ten lepers I healed, only one came back to say thank you. Only *one*—and I am thinking of him, as I am thinking of you now, when you might be the one who comes back to thank Me for setting you free. For your sake I do this. For *your* sake I endure this beating. For *your* sake I endure this mockery. I will remain the silent Lamb led to the slaughter,

"For like sheep you have ALL gone astray and will go astray..."
Isaiah 53:6

The noise of the crowd began to dim, as the surreal setting of My torturous lashing was prepared right before My very eyes. The sinister darkness that pressed in around Me, proved an ominous albatross, much heavier than the clouds brewing. The portentous doom contained the sin of humanity— ugliness, murder, rape, crimes of violence, robbery, greed, gossip, envy, lust, abuse, child abuse, jealousy, adultery, rage and revenge.

The soldiers could have simply scourged Me, but they began with stripping Me first, tearing away My most humble, blood-stained clothing. As they tore it from Me, parts of My skin, stuck to the clothing, ripped to cause even deeper lacerations into My body.

Perhaps the reason to strip Me naked, was to make the men feel more powerful. They had armor on—thick metal. I had only a thin layer of skin. Skin is the largest organ on the body. It is a delicate membrane of molecules, alive, and is extremely sensitive to pain. I was fully God in a fully human form.

Had they known the heart of God was beating inside of My fragile chest—the Heart which beats universal love in perfect time throughout all of eternity? If they had known, they may have stopped dead in their sandals. They may have bowed before Me, for soldiers understand a clear line of command.

Unseen by the crowd, the religious leaders, and the soldiers, the heavenly angels poised around Me. They remained motionless, at My Father's command, weeping as they watched the fallen angels, the demons, along with satan, close in around Me. I heard the demons mocking Me like cacklers in a crowd, as the people continued to yell, "Crucify Him! Crucify Him!"

The demons soared with strength. They puffed up their chests and gloated with new-found glee—given to them only for *this* hour. Just as satan had entered Judas when He had betrayed Me, satan had only a limited time to dwell in Judas. Satan and his fallen angels have only a limited time on Earth. Satan knows this.

The broad-shouldered soldiers were pumped up with adrenaline on account of the cheering crowd and after Pilate's orders to scourge Me, they jumped into action. Not that they were eager to get on with it, but, like trained pawns in the hands of a grandmaster cheating on a rigged board, they did what they were told and when they were told.

Alone at night, with their own thoughts, it might be hard to rally a man of muscle to do such a deed, but here, with the masses ranting in their support of the whipping, the soldiers found even greater strength. Besides, the Jewish people meant nothing to them. I meant nothing to them. They trained daily, through rain or shine, thick or thin, beating their bodies into the strength of iron—just for a task like this.

I was not afraid of them as they surrounded me, much like hungry lions surround a helpless lamb. I was the Lamb of God destined to die for their sins. It was My Father's will. I was to be the perfect sacrifice for humanity. As the soldiers hovered over Me, whips poised, they did not know that I was the Lion of the Tribe of Judah. They did not know that if I had chosen to roar at that very instant with My mighty voice of many waters, they would have fallen flat at My feet instead.

But as the clock of destiny struck the countdown of My final hour, I was in obedient submission to My Father. My Father had given Me a mission, and I would complete it this day. In only a few hours, I would be lifted high upon a cross for all to see. I would even feel forsaken even by My own Father.

The soldiers would not look in My eyes. Compassion was not one of their strong suits. If they found weakness in the victim, it would only interrupt their deep-seated training of obedience. They could not show mercy at all cost. If an ounce of kindness or pity rose up in their psyche, they would not have been able to carry out the barbaric task set before them. If they felt even a tinge of sympathy or tenderness, the brutality they were exerting would prove to be absurd, and they might retreat from their savage duties. So, to completely avoid empathy, they succumbed to absolute callousness, which caused them to be even more heartless and sadistic than was necessary.

If they did, however, look into My eyes, they would have found compassion, not weakness. They would have found perfect love, not fear. They were, in fact, the ones who were afraid. Any person knows they should not hurt another person. It is written in the absolute law of a human heart. But cultures, groups, mobs, and even a tribe can often convince a person that it is not only acceptable, but necessary to commit violence against another person.

Today—the violence committed by all of humanity, past, present and future would be whipped onto My back.

Before I was mercilessly beaten with the scourge—thirty-nine lashes by the hand of the strongest of the soldiers—the soldiers led Me past the legionnaire who held the scourge tightly in his hands. Just the sight of the scourge often made strong men faint—two leather thongs loaded with lead, spikes and bones, in order to rip the skin from the body, and in this case rip My skin from My body.

I could feel the rough, enormous hands of the soldier who now took My arms and tied them to the pillar—not that he had to tie My arms. I was not struggling. He did not need to cinch the rope so tight. He could have loosened them in pity for Me to ease My burdens. He would get no fight from Me. But instead of easing up, he wrapped the rope tighter and tighter, until My veins were popping out. He was unaware that he tightened them in order to solidify his own actions, to somehow justify himself, to convince himself that I *was* a dangerous criminal after all—one who needed to be tightly secured. My shoulders screamed in pain as they were pulled to the point of being out of joint.

The flogging will begin now.

I am willing to take the lashes in order for *you* to be healed one day. By My stripes you can be healed... for I was thinking of you, as I am thinking of you now.

As his hand raised to implement the first lash, the crowd silenced for a timeless inhale. It might seem justified to beat someone, to punish them, or even kill them, until you see it happening before your eyes and you pause for a brief moment, wondering if you made the right decision.

As the bits of bones and the spikes from the cat-o'-nine tails ripped into My flesh, it felt like the claws of a huge hawk or vulture tearing into its prey. As I cowered beneath the sheer pain, I focused on My precious followers, who throughout the years to come will be tortured, burned at the stake, mocked, beaten and thrown into prison. I was praying for My followers, especially for those who will not understand why the journey with Me has to be so hard at times.

"ONE," the soldier who would count the blows cried out.

As the countdown of My flagellation began, known as the "half death" which could easily cause disfigurement and serious trauma, as pieces of skin and muscle were ripped from My body, causing Me to approach a state of hypovolemic shock due to the loss of blood, I was thinking of the assailants, praying for them, just as I am thinking of you and praying for you now...

The glory of God is *not* the glory of man. My kingdom is *not* of this Earth. My kingdom is *NOT* of this Earth.

"Do not lay up for yourselves treasures on Earth,
Where moth and rust destroy and where thieves break in and steal;
But lay up for yourselves treasures in heaven,

Where neither moth nor rust destroys
And where thieves do not break in and steal.
For where your treasure is, there your heart will be also."
Matthew 6:19-20

My heart was with you during the scourging. You are My treasure. Many times you will lose the primary focus of My kingdom while you journey for a short time on the Earth. You will forget what is really important. You cannot serve God and money. You cannot take anything with you when your body expires. Store up for yourselves treasures in *heaven*. Where your treasure is, there will be your heart. You are My treasure — My heart is with you.

Each venomous lash on My back would open the door a little bit more to enable a soul to enter into the kingdom of heaven. My eye was single, My Body, though being tortured, was full of light — focused on My Father's will.

"TWO!" I thought of My prayer before the last supper, before the countdown to the cross, when I pleaded with My Father to set apart our precious followers — those who did follow, who are following, who will follow — to each of their own deaths — misunderstood, mocked and ridiculed for following Me.

"And now I am no more in the world, but these are in the world,
And I come to Thee.
Holy Father, keep through thine own name those whom thou hast given Me,
That they may be one, as we are..." John 17:11

"THREE!" This blow curled the flesh on My back, leaving My body with long, deep wounds. Blood was everywhere. My precious blood, blood that heals diseases and raises the dead, was being poured out onto the stones of Jerusalem. I am becoming the Temple.

I remained steadfast to focus on the JOY set before Me. You are My joy. Your precious soul is My crown.

I lifted My eyes up to heaven to seek strength from the cloud of witnesses — Moses, Elijah, Abraham, Isaac, Ruth, Deborah, Isaiah were all cheering Me on — to be the author and finisher of faith for all time. They applauded Me and encouraged Me to remember you — My crown, just as they will cheer you on while you run the race to win the high prize of the calling of God.

"Wherefore seeing you are compassed about

With so great a cloud of witnesses,
Lay aside every weight, and the sin which so easily besets you,
And run with patience the race that is set before you."
Hebrews 12:1

"FOUR!" I quoted My own prayer I had prayed for My disciples, to keep Me on this narrow track...

"Father, the hour is come; glorify Your Son, Jesus,
That I would also glorify You..."

"FIVE!"

"For You have given ME power over all flesh,
That I should give eternal life to as many as You have given ME..."

"SIX!"

"And this is life eternal, that they might know You,
Yahuweh, the only true God..."

"SEVEN!"

"And know Me, Messiah Jesus, whom You have sent..."

"EIGHT!" The whip encircled My neck, and temporarily stuck, like a snake sent from hell itself, to choke the very life out of Me. I gagged. It took My breath away for only a few seconds, but it seemed like an eternity. I staggered against the post.

For a moment, frozen in time, the crowd held their breath. "Surely He might die right now," some thought.

Pilate also staggered under the weight of this particular blow. He clutched his own throat. As the whip circled back around My neck, taking My skin with it, Pilate scratched deep into his skin without knowing it; until blood was in his fingernails. His hands were soiled with his own blood. "I need to wash my hands again," he thought.

"NINE!"

"Focus. Narrow is the way," I said to Myself, after I caught My breath. "Focus..."

"I have glorified You on Earth, O Lord.
I have finished the work which You gave Me to do..."

"TEN!" The crowd reeled. Some swooned. Others got up to leave. This was *way* too much. The stronger, more stubborn members of the crowd stayed on. One of the soldiers started to convulse as if to vomit. The air began to stink like sulphur—sin personified in a stench. The smell of nervous sweat from the crowd and the soldiers permeated the atmosphere along with the smell of My blood. The Chief Priests and Scribes were turning their faces away, hiding their faces from Me, just as Isaiah had prophesied, as if it could erase the blood that now stained their white garments. Even Pilate felt faint in his seat of high power.

I was God in human form, yet I did not use any of My supernatural powers. I felt every blow. And with each blow, I was thinking of you...

"ELEVEN!"

"And now, O Father, glorify Me with Your Holy Self and
With the glory which I had with You before the world was..."

I continued to quote the prayer in My mind. It helped Me to concentrate on the glory of the Father, which is not the glory of the Earth. I had set My mind on the Kingdom of God so that when you are weary on your pilgrim journey on Earth, you will be strengthened in your mind to fixate on the kingdom of God; for I was thinking of you, as I am thinking of you now...

"TWELVE!"

I reeled. My body writhed with pain searing through My muscles. I thought of My disciples, as I continued to pray...

"I have manifested Your Name to the ones
Whom You have given Me, who have come out of the world unto Yourself,
O Father. You gave them to Me and they have kept Your Word..."

I thought about My Beloved Peter who would be martyred upside down on a cross for My sake. I thought of the countless martyrs throughout generations who would suffer for Me and even die for Me. Many will lose their children and their family members. If they suffer for Me, they will reign with Me.

"THIRTEEN!"

"Now they have known that all things
You have given Me Are of You.
For I have given to them, the words which You gave Me
And they have received them.
They have surely known that I came from You
And they have believed that You sent Me.
I pray for them..."

I was weeping in My spirit now, not because of the intense suffering I was going through, but for the persecution I knew My disciples and those who would follow Me would endure, for centuries upon centuries, even to the end of the age. I pray for them...

> *"I pray not for the world, but for those whom You have given Me,*
> *O Father, for they are Yours. All Mine are Yours,*
> *And Yours are mine and I am glorified in them..."*

The glory that is Mine will be theirs as each of them walk through their own valleys of the shadow of death. Their faces will reflect the glory of the Lord. Each wound I will bear with them, as I bear their wounds now. Each sorrow I will carry, as I will carry their sorrows to the cross this day.

"FOURTEEN!"

"Father, strengthen Me to endure *their* pain," I groaned in My Spirit to My Father in Heaven.

> *"When I am no more in the world,*
> *My disciples will be in the world.*
> *I come to You, Holy Father.*
> *Keep through Your Name those who You have given Me,*
> *That they may be one as we are One..."*

"FIFTEEN!"

"SIXTEEN!"

"SEVENTEEN!"

"EIGHTEEN!"

"NINETEEN!"

"TWENTY!"

Some people could not bear to keep watching the spectacle of My body being marred, My face drenched with blood, sweat, tears. My lips are chapped, bleeding. My skin is hanging from my body in the most grotesque manner. My knees are shaking beyond control. I am in shock. My body is groaning, begging, to fall to the earth to find relief, but I am tied to this pillar. My arms are weak, exhausted and strained. My muscles, veins, nerves are exposed where the whip has driven into My flesh.

I could summon legions of angels, mighty and powerful. One angel, alone, would be enough to terrify this crowd and send the soldiers running. I felt the wickedness of the religious leaders—their hearts were much like this whip. They shred their people just as they shred Me, laying ridiculous rules upon them, rule upon rule, line upon line, precept upon precept. "They feed themselves and let their sheep starve. I will come

again to judge the shepherds. I will also judge between the fat sheep and the lean. I am the Good Shepherd that will feed My people."
Ezekiel 34; John 10

I could take My whip again, right now, and drive the religious leaders away from Me, those who do not rule in love, truth, righteousness and mercy. I could drive them out just as I drove out the sellers in the temple in Jerusalem when...

"I found those who sold oxen and sheep and doves,
And the money changers doing business,
I made a whip of cords, I drove them all out of the temple,
With the sheep and the oxen, I poured out the changers' money and
overturned the tables. I said to those who sold doves,
'Take these things away! Do not make My Father's house a house of
merchandise!'" *So the Jews answered and said to Me,*
"What sign do You show to us, since You do these things?"

It is then I answered and said to them...

"Destroy this temple, and in three days I will raise it up."

"It has taken forty-six years to build this temple, and will You raise it up in three days?" They answered Me, but they did not know—*"I was speaking of My body."*

I said to them...

"My house shall be called the house of prayer;
But you have made it a den of thieves." Matthew 21:12-13

The zeal of My Father's house had consumed Me. The false leaders deserved the whip that was falling on My back today, just as the buyers and sellers deserved the whip, as I overturned their tables in the temple, but instead—it was *I* taking the whipping for them so that, in My obedience unto death, I would become the Temple in order that no unclean person or thing could ever rob the people of the Temple again. The Temple of My body would be the only Temple for true worship from now and forever more.

If you are a leader in a false religion, I say, "Woe to you." You had better know that you *know* that you *know* before you teach someone a religious doctrine. As the whip kept striking, I was thinking of you. If you have been taught wrongly by another or if you have been caught in a web of religious lies, you can call on My name, Jesus. You can come freely into

My Temple and worship Me in spirit and truth. Repent. Take up your cross and follow Me.

As blow "TWENTY-ONE!" fell upon Me, I pressed back into My prayer for My own expressed in John 17, carrying each of their blows on My own back.

"While I was with them in the world, I kept them in Your Name.
Those that You gave Me, I have kept.
None of them will be lost, except for the son of perdition, Judas,
In order that the scriptures will be fulfilled.
And, now, Father, I come to You. I spoke to My own in the world,
That they might have joy in themselves. I have given them Your word.
I have given them Myself.
The world will hate them, because they are not of the world,
Even as I am not of the world…"

"TWENTY-TWO!" How is it, that I am I still standing? I am not really. I'm hanging by a thread. My body is frayed beyond repair, as I continued to pray for you…

"Father, I do not pray that You will take them out of the world,
But that You will keep them from evil."

"TWENTY-THREE!"

"They are not of the world, even as I am not of the world.
Set them apart, Yahuweh, with Your truth; Your Word is truth.
I am the Torah made flesh—The Way, the Truth and the Life.
As You sent me into the world, even so, I have sent them into the world
And will send them.
For their sakes, I set Myself apart,
That they might be set apart and made holy through the Truth…"

"TWENTY-FOUR!"

"I am not simply praying for my current disciples,
But for those who will believe on Me through their testimony.
I pray that they will be one as You, Father, are in Me and I am in You.
I pray that they will also be one in Us.
I pray that the world may believe that You have sent Me…"

"TWENTY-FIVE!"

It is past the point of ridiculous now. Why do they have to keep the scourge going? Why thirty-nine lashes? Surely an eternity has passed since last night, much like the forty days of fasting without food or water in the desert times one million. Although the pain is the most intense physical pain I have ever endured, it is nothing compared to the anguish of a soul darkened with sin—facing the wrath of a righteous and holy God with no hope of a savior. I am blameless, spotless. I have no sin, so even though My flesh is torn from my bones, I am pure light, through and through. I have no darkness in Me.

"TWENTY-SIX!"

"TWENTY-SEVEN!"

"TWENTY-EIGHT!"

"TWENTY-NINE!"

Aaaaaagh! I wanted to scream out! I slumped against the post. One of the soldiers abruptly pulled me back to My feet. They turned My body around to whip the other side, since there was no skin left on my back to scourge. I heard the lambs bleating in the distance, getting ready to be prepared for the Passover. Soon they would be skinned—their skin pulled off of their unblemished bodies, just as My skin is being pulled off of My unblemished body. But I did not scream. I kept silent, blood streaming into My eyes, My nostrils, My ears, and My mouth.

In My heart, I held you. In My eternal heart, I knew you would weep one day in your own pain and suffering. During that time, turn to Me —the stripes on My back, which I am enduring now, will make you whole —for I was thinking of you, as I am thinking of you now…

Life is in the blood, and it is My Blood which will make you whole. This is the glory of God, the life that I give for the world.

"The Glory, Lord, that You gave me, I will give to them,

That they may be one even as We are one.

I in them, and You in Me, that they may be made perfect in one.

I pray that they would know You love them as You have loved Me…"

"THIRTY!" With this stripe, I heal you of your diseases. Call upon Me and I will answer. Ask, it will be given to you. Seek and you will find. Knock and the door will be opened to you. When you ask, believe. Your faith will make you whole. And those who die without the promises will be those whom the world is not worthy of…

"THIRTY-ONE!"

"Father, I will that they, who You have given Me,

Be with Me were I am; that they may behold My glory,

Which You have given Me,

For You loved Me before the foundation of the world…"
"THIRTY-TWO!"
   "Righteous Father, the world has not known You,
But I have known You and my disciples have known that You have sent
Me…"
"THIRTY-THREE!"
      "I have declared to them…
"THIRTY-FOUR!" I am breathing heavily. I can barely think…
"THIRTY-FIVE!"
      "I will declare that…"
"THIRTY-SIX!"
      "The Love in which You have loved Me…"
"THIRTY-SEVEN!"
      "May be in them…"
"THIRTY-EIGHT!"
      "And I in them…"
"THIRTY-NINE!"
      "Forever and ever,"
      "Amen."
      John 17

I slumped into a bloody ball. I was beyond exhausted now, but I was still thinking of you, as I am thinking of you now. When you are exhausted on your journey, when you weary of helping others or enduring persecution, I have borne your burdens. I have carried your pains. Your wounds are engraved in Mine; you who bear the marks of the Lord will be greatly honored. My wounds will heal your wounds. With life-giving blood, I pour into your weary soul the power of *Yahuweh*.

In Me, the mystery of the Messiah, you possess all things—

As the whip wreaked havoc with My body, I was carrying you, just as I was holding the universe in the palm of My hand. My body was shaken, but My plans were not. I was carrying you, as I am carrying you now, just as I am bearing your burdens until I come again in the clouds.

      "I will never leave you, nor forsake you."
      Hebrews 13:5
"The world does not know Me, the world will not know you,
But you know Me. Be of good cheer, I have overcome the world."
      John 16:33

158

At this point I collapsed on the ground, but I will rise. I will rise again and conquer death for all time.

Believe in Me and you shall never die.
John 11:26

Setting...
Back at the Praetorium

Matthew 27

With the manipulation of the priests, the rant of the assembly, the desire of Pilate to uphold his reputation before his people, and the troop of Roman soldiers willing and obedient to carry out their orders, the stage for My ultimate spectacle was completed. The demented crowd syndrome, mixed with fear, peer pressure, egos, and brute strength, had kicked into full gear.

I had just endured the most brutal of tortures, yet I was the One who felt sorry for *them*. I knew what I had to do, but they did not know. Later, at the point of My death, when I will cry out to My Father, many of them will bow on bended knee and know that they have killed a righteous man.

But today, I was to be slaughtered, not worshipped. It was necessary to bear curse of humanity upon Myself so that I could absolve your curse. When you have been mocked, beaten or scourged—physically, mentally or emotionally, I have experienced suffering before you. I am alone in my suffering, but you will never be alone. I will have gone before you to prepare eternal paradise where there will be no more pain.

"I will never leave you nor forsake you," for after all, I was thinking of you, as I am thinking of you now...

"When you are weary, I will cause you to rest in green pastures.
I will lead you beside still waters.
I will restore your soul. I will lead you in My path for righteousness sake.
In your deepest valley, I am with you, even in the shadow of death.
You will fear no evil.
My rod and My staff will comfort you.
In the presence of your enemies, I will prepare a table for you.
I will anoint your head with oil.

Your cup will graciously run over.
Goodness and mercy will follow you
And you will dwell in My house forever." Psalm 23

When you find yourself surrounded by a crowd demanding your crucifixion after they have already beaten you, "Come away with Me." This crowd could be coworkers who ridicule you or members of your own family or your government, or even your religion who persecute you.

Come away—you can find a quiet place of rest in Me.

Come away, My beloved. Come away from the noise, the confusion. Come rest by My still waters. Come lie down in My green pastures. I am thinking of you. I feel your need for deep, lasting rest and peace, just as I could feel the needs of each hard heart surrounding Me now, even while they shouted out obscenities and hurled insults at Me.

One of the soldiers who looked like a captain was twisting large thorns into the shape of a crown. I could see the malice in his heart, as he went to great lengths in order to make fun of Me. The mangling of the thorns in his huge, gnarly hands reflected his twisted heart—savage and cruel. He, perhaps, had no idea of what drove him to be so intent on crafting this odious crown of corruption. When he was a boy, he wanted to be a sculptor, but after years of hardship growing up with a harsh father, then serving in the heartless Roman army, he had long sense forgotten this dream.

I knew the motivating force behind his actions. Hurting people hurt people. He was tired of the abuse of his ruthless leaders. He had become the strongest and toughest of the soldiers in order to protect himself. But his heart was bitter. He could protect his body, with physical strength, but he could not protect his heart. A bitter root had developed in his heart, and tree of the rotten fruit of malice had formed inside of him to defile those around him.

Years ago, after each sun had set, he went to bed fuming with hurt and anger after his father's severe beatings. The festering of his wounds gave the *real* enemy of his soul a foothold for this bitter root to grow. This anger only grew more intense when he joined the Roman army. His temper made him a quick fighter, and he became one of the most revered soldiers, but the rage inside of him, welled up like a smoldering volcano. As he formed the warped crown, the heat inside of him grew more intense, and the explosion was soon to be released with full vengeance—on My head.

Here I was, weak and helpless, just as he once was. He had vowed as a boy, to never be weak again, and he hated the sight of the pathetic man cowering before him who called Himself the Son of God.

"Do not let the sun go down while you are angry,
And do not give the devil a foothold." Ephesians 4:26-27

I knew the one, the evil one, who was *really* the one mocking Me behind this soldier's stiff, unshaven jaw, the one driving the force of his fury. Continually over time, satan will try to convince people that *he* has the power, but he has *no* power.

ALL power has been given to Me—in heaven and on earth.
Matthew 28:18

In a few hours, I will make an open display of victory over the enemy. The seed which came through Eve, continued on through the scarlet thread of redemption to My virgin mother, Mary, will crush the lying serpent's head forever. I will be obedient unto death. My death will be the victory. Surely, My death is a more powerful expression of My love than My resurrection. I am God. It is *easy* for Me to live. I am life. I came to give life, and more abundantly, but to *die* for the sins of humanity. This is My greatest act of perfect LOVE.

Forgiveness is the pivotal point of My message. Many false gods will vie for your love and devotion, but only ONE God will die for you.

One day, when you know you need a Savior—I will be there.

Pilate hoped that the scourging would be enough to satisfy the crowd, the Scribes and the Pharisees. But as the blood-thirsty crowd saw the blood running down My ripped face, My torn chest and back, they only seemed to want more. "Crucify Him! Crucify Him!"

My sacrifice would not be complete without My death. Just like the blood of each slaughtered lamb, applied to the doorposts in Egypt, saved the first-born of every family from the angel of death. Now, My blood can be spread over anyone's heart. Anyone who calls on My name.

"I came to My own,
And those who were My own did not receive Me.
But as many as received Me, to them I gave the right
To become children of God, even to those who believe in My name."
John 1:11-12

The soldiers barbarically tossed the scarlet robe over My torn shoulders in order to mock My royalty. They pressed the cloth into My wounds to cause extra anguish, embedding the robe into My sores.

As they clothed Me, they may have felt the power of My mantle of authority which reigns over all of the Earth – the same power which could blast the clothes right off of them — the power that could strip their human hearts, leaving them as naked as I was, but it was not the time for this power. My people needed a humble Savior who would be humiliated for them so that when they realize their own humiliation, when they are stripped bare, with nothing to cover their sin, they have Me, a Savior who has borne their humiliation.

Most of the soldiers were young men — strong, trained warriors, yet so scared underneath, so frightened. Often the toughest men are the most timid inside. Their strength becomes their weakness, because they can hide momentarily behind a strong physique. Those who are physically weak live with a daily realization that is it God who must help them be strong. In their weakness, My strength is made perfect.

Today, it is important that the soldiers do not recognize Me. If they did, they might take compassion on Me, they might even try to save Me, release Me from My bonds and find a way to get Me out of here; but no one must save Me today. It is I who will save the world. As it is written…

"For He made Him who knew no sin to be sin for us, that we might become the righteousness of God in Him." 2 Corinthians 5:21

At this time, the grotesque crown of thorns came into full view. The pain up to this point had been excruciating beyond belief. I did not know how I could bear any more. Anyone who had known Me before would not recognize Me now. The soldier grinned maliciously as he carried the tangled mess of thorns with its long spikes and lifted it high above his head, showing his wicked craftsmanship to the horde.

He callously brought it over to Me and held it above My head, much with the look of a joker on his face. The crowd rose to their feet and clapped even louder as he placed it as a crown on My head. The soldiers rallied to help him slam the malicious crown into My skull. The blood streamed down My face, into My eyes. I could barely see. My blood-soaked robe was hot and heavy. I staggered, as my body shook uncontrollably from the pain.

The soldiers mocked Me and ridiculed Me as they pried My fingers open to shove the fake staff into My right hand. "Hail, King of the Jews!" "Hail, King of the Jews!"

With the crown of thorns, the scarlet robe, and the staff, I looked much like a sad clown in a circus. What was so ironic, yet so fatally true, was that before them did stand a king—the King of the Universe. The world rarely recognizes greatness in a person until after they die. This is how it will be in My case. This is how it will be with countless men and women who will come after Me in My name. The world did not recognize Me. The world will not recognize My disciples. Many true saints will give themselves for Me. These are the flaming pillars who make up the structure of My true church. These will suffer martyrdom, even by the hands of the organized "church." From this day on, there is only one temple, Me.

To those who are perishing, My way seems foolish, but to those who are saved, My way is powerful. The foolish now were before Me, around Me, behind Me, spitting on Me, cursing Me from outside the gate. Some of the soldiers knelt before Me to exemplify their mocking even further, while they continued to shout, "Hail, King of the Jews!"

The one who had made the crown of thorns now stood back with his arms crossed to view his work with deplorable pleasure. A brief memory surfaced as he looked on his heinous work of art, now driven into My bleeding skull. He remembered playing with a branch when he was a boy, twisting it together with other branches, to make his first work of art— a nest for a baby bird who had fallen from a tree.

"*Why* am I thinking of this now?" He thought to himself as the crowd and the Praetorium faded into the backdrop.

He remembered how he felt as he gently laid the baby bird in the nest and settled it back in the olive tree. There were blue bird eggs on the ground, too. He lifted the fragile shells and with child-like hope placed them back in their nest. The broken shell of the baby bird lay on the ground. He affectionately put it into his pocket and waited behind a bush, watching until the mother bird found her baby and the eggs in her newly placed nest. He had felt so proud. The memory jogged something within him, so tender so true. This was before he became bitter and angry.

It was at this moment, when his tough shell of the beast he had become, began to crack like the shell of that tender egg.

"What's happening to me? Why is everyone is staring at me?" he thought. He gazed all around, but no one was paying any attention to him. "What's wrong with me? I must be going mad."

He then looked up at Me. I lifted My eyes, with blood pouring over them, to meet his gaze. He had felt proud a moment ago with the crowd cheering him on, but all of a sudden he did not feel as proud of his work anymore.

"Why is He looking at Me like that?" his thoughts stammered to himself.

Perhaps I looked much like the baby bird, but instead of saving it, he was hurting it? Tears welled up in his eyes... He blinked many times to keep them from falling down his face, thus being shamed him in public. He cast his eyes to the ground and did not look up anymore.

I was not thinking of the pain that was set before Me any longer, I was thinking of him. He would lift his eyes to Me again one day in prayer. At that moment, forgiveness will flow to him from the blood pouring down My face. His salvation would be sealed because I could see inside to his heart of repentance.

I lifted My eyes to heaven. I was not thinking of him anymore. I was thinking of you, just as I am thinking of you now... when you have twisted a lie that caused hurt instead of made a beautiful nest of truth to heal.

All throughout the coming years on Earth, even after My death and resurrection, people, much like those present today will continue to mock Me. I do not look like a king. I will not look like a king reigning from My cross, bloody and beaten, beyond human repair. But what does a true king look like? Does he look like Caesar?

A true king is a servant of all. During My greatest humiliation, I was thinking of you, just as I am thinking of you now... When you are ruled by a wicked ruler and the people in your nation are oppressed, you have a righteous ruler you can call upon – Messiah Jesus, the Savior of the world. I am with you in your season of humiliation or torture, when no one recognizes you and Me in you—when they hate you, cast you out of their churches and synagogues, disown you, beat you, dismember you, or even kill you. Their faulty institutions are threatened when you simply point out the *one* narrow way which leads to eternal life—Jesus.

Some people will label Me a higher power, a prophet, a guru, or a good man. All of these are partially true, but not *the* truth. If you strip Me of My power of being God on Earth, then when you are desperately lost and you need power, you will not have that power. Power is not found in a mere man, but in the name of your Lord, the name above every name, Jesus, the Messiah.

"I am *HE*," I could have said, and watched the soldiers fall to the ground, but instead, they puffed their chests out, grabbed the staff they had given Me and beat me over the head. The staff only served to pound the thorns deeper into My skull. It was almost impossible to think now, but with every bit of strength I had in Me, I was thinking of you. I was thinking of times of persecution that you will endure, when you will be in your own torture chamber, where your physical or emotional pain will seem to be beyond what you can bear—when you are tempted to deny Me —when you wonder if it is all true—when the words of the liar will beat against your skull... "See, you trusted in Jesus, and look how much you have suffered."

When you have claimed to be a prophet and now you are being burned at the stake, it is at this time I am thinking of you. Don't shrink back. Be faithful unto death.

"And they overcame satan by the blood of the Lamb and by the word
Of their testimony, and they did not love their lives to the death."
Revelation 12:11

I could not see anymore because of the blood running into My eyes, but I must remain focused on the joy that is set before Me. The joy I cannot see with My human eyes. I will not look on what I see, but what I do not see. Set My site on the finish line—heaven.

There can be no flinching, no second guessing, no show of weakness, no sign of breaking. I must go through with His plan. I have put My hand to the plow for My Kingdom and I will not look back, so when you have put your hand to the plow to sow into the kingdom of God, you will have a Savior who has gone before you, without retreating in the face of pain. You will find strength in My sacrifice to not look back. I will steady Myself with roots—unshakable roots which grow from the beginning, wrap the globe, and hold the universe unto the end of eternity. With these strong roots, I will find the courage and tenacity to remain faithful to the end.

I am the author and finisher of your faith. I was thinking of you, as I am thinking of you now.

When I am lifted up, I will draw all people to Myself.

Setting...
Back at Pilate's — Pilates last plea.

John 19:5-17

One of the soldiers moved forward to hand the staff back to Me. At least it looked like he wanted to hand it to Me, but instead, with one last, mocking grin, he brought it down upon My head and then passed it to his comrades. They proceeded to strike Me in the face. My face, now marred beyond recognition fulfilled Isaiah's prophecies, "His face is marred beyond human likeness..."

When the beating finally stopped, Pilate cringed as he presented Me to the crowd. "Behold the Man!"

"Surely, the crowd would relent. Surely, the religious leaders would stop this madness as they witness the shattered remains of a man standing before them," Pilate thought, as he held his breath for what seemed to be an eternal time continuum.

As in a nightmare that does not end, the crowd continued, "Crucify Him!"

"Take Him yourself," Pilate retorted. "And crucify Him!"

The Chief Scribes and Pharisees answered, "We have a law, that He should be put to death, because He called Himself the Son of God, equal with God."

I *was* God. I am God. I am that I am. Standing before them was the very God who made the heavens and the Earth. My Father and I are one. All throughout history, until the end of the age, men and women will decide that I am not God. They will write books about My life as a prophet, but they will not believe who I really am. Who I said I am.

These false prophets will influence others to not believe in Me, therefore causing little ones to stumble. They will strip Me of power, or so they think. There will supposedly be new information about Me that is uncovered to prove that I am not God — but throughout the centuries, men, women and children will come to Me and *know* Me. These precious followers will understand My redemptive power.

The powerless do not like it when someone else is powerful. It bothers them because they know their hearts are foolish and dark. Because of their impotence, they surround themselves with big words and high degrees of knowledge where they esteem each other's outsides, without ever cleaning the muck on the inside. These teachers are empty bags of water. They are not able to give you a drink of pure living water of *Yahuweh*, because they are not drinking from the well of salvation.

> *"These people are blemishes at your love feasts,*
> *Eating with you without the slightest qualm—*
> *Shepherds who feed only themselves.*
> *They are clouds without rain, blown along by the wind;*
> *Autumn trees, without fruit and uprooted—twice dead.*
> *They are wild waves of the sea, foaming up their shame; wandering stars,*
> *For whom blackest darkness has been reserved forever."*
> *Jude 1:12*

There will *always* be these people, until there is no more time. You will know them by their fruits. Remember...

> *"The fruits of the spirit are love, joy, peace, forbearance, kindness,*
> *Goodness, faithfulness, gentleness and self-control.*
> *Against such things there is no law." Galatians 5:22-23*
> *"Anyone who does not love, does not know Me, for I am love."*
> *1 John 4:8*

This is how you will know if they are My disciples—if they have the fruits of the Spirit and they love *Yahuweh* and all people. "If someone loves Me with all of their heart and loves their neighbor as themselves, there are no commandments greater than these." *Mark 12:30-31*

As I taught in the temple, I answered the religious leaders who did not recognize Me...

> *"I said, 'You know neither Me nor My Father; if you knew Me,*
> *You would know My Father also. I go away, and you will seek Me,*
> *And will die in your sin; where I am going, you cannot come.*
> *You are from below, I am from above;*
> *You are of this world, I am not of this world.*
> *Therefore I said to you that you will die in your sins;*
> *For unless you believe that I am He, you will die in your sins.'"*

John 8:19-24-25

They said to Me, "Who are You?"

The religious leaders had seen Me teaching daily in the countryside, feeding the five thousand, healing the sick, and raising the dead. Why did they not recognize Me? If they had *known* the Father, they would have *known* Me.

When I said, "I am going away, and you will look for me, and you will die in your sin. Where I go you cannot come," the religious leaders murmured amongst themselves. "'Will He kill Himself?' Is that why He says, 'Where I go you cannot come?'"

So often, that is how it is with religious leaders. They cannot understand spiritual truth, because they are so deeply embedded into their own doctrines.

I told them, *"You are from below; I am from above. You are of this world; I am not of this world. I told you that you would die in your sins; if you do not believe that I am He, you will die in your sins." John 8:24*

They still could not understand. They will not even understand after they have lifted Me up to be crucified. They do not know that I only do what pleases My Father. They do not know Me *nor* My Father. My Father and I are one.

Many of My people, who are *humble* of heart, will believe Me, which is how it will be throughout centuries to come.

"Blessed are the pure in heart, for they shall see God."

Matthew 5:8

The proud cannot see Me. The religious leaders argued with Me. They could have received Me as the Son of God and spared their people years of hardship being scattered throughout the Earth like vagabonds, but their pride had blinded them. They would rather establish their own righteousness than accept the righteousness of the Messiah.

I told them, "If they would listen to My teaching, they would be My disciples. They would know the Truth and the Truth would set them free." But instead of listening and accepting Me as a child would, with a pure heart and pure motives, the religious leaders stammered back and forth, referring to their traditions, rather than realizing the day of their visitation from their own Messiah.

"We are Abraham's descendants and have never been slaves of anyone. How can you say that we will be set free?" They retorted.

171

I responded that they are indeed slaves to sin. Slaves have no permanent place in the family. On the other hand, a son belongs to the family forever.

"If the Son sets you free, you are free indeed." John 8:38

I said to them, "I know that you are Abraham's descendants, yet you seek to kill Me, the one sent from *Yahuweh*. You have no room for Me, for My Word, even though I have been with the Father and He with Me. You are doing what you have heard from your father."

"You are of your father the devil,
And the lusts of your father you will do. He was a murderer from the
Beginning, and abode not in the truth, because there is no truth in him.
When he speaks a lie, he speaks of his own:
For he is a liar, and the father of it." John 8:44

They stubbornly replied, "Abraham is our father. We are not illegitimate children."

I wish I could have pierced their petrified hearts with My truth, but spirit cannot communicate with flesh. They were dead in their sins. I wanted to weep for them, but it was for their followers I had the greater compassion. Leaders come under greater judgment. It must be so.

Again, they clamored, "We are not illegitimate children, the only Father we have is God, himself."

I replied, *"If God were your Father, you would love Me, for I have come from God. I have not come on My own. Why is this not clear to you? It is not clear because you cannot hear what I say. The ears of your heart are deaf because you belong to your father, the devil, and it is your father, the liar, who wishes for Me to die, And you will carry out his desires. He was a murderer from the beginning, not holding to the truth, for there is no truth in him. He is the father of lies. The reason you cannot hear me, is that you do not belong to God." from John 8 (paraphrased)*

It is so now, and it will be so throughout generations. Many of My chosen people of Israel will crucify Me over and over again. Yet, some of My own *will* receive Me as their Messiah, and I will be a Savior to them. They will run to tell the rabbis and leaders of their synagogues with great joy and elation. When they speak of Me and My salvation, they will be driven out of the synagogues, temples and mosques—beheaded, stoned to death, hung on crosses or burned at the stake.

As the hardness of the religious leaders' hearts came down on Me like the staff they were beating Me with, I was thinking of My followers. You might not be martyred after you give your life to Me, but you may feel ostracized from your family and be driven out of your circle of friends. When you are ridiculed for believing in Me, I am thinking of you.

The hardness of the hearts of the Chief Scribes and Pharisees made Pilate afraid also. If I, Jesus, who stood before him, truly committed blasphemy and Pilate did not succumb to their angry cries for My blood, the people would turn on him. Pilate could not have that happen. He thought again, if he could persuade Me to give up My claim, then this whole filthy incident could blow over before midday.

"Where do you come from?" Pilate asked Me again. I remained silent. I could have said anything to save My life at that moment, yet I am the Truth and there is no lie in Me. I cannot lie as the religious leaders do. The time it took for Me to *not* answer encapsulated the last three years of My ministry on Earth. *Now* was the time of My salvation, and I would not give in to any ploy of man.

Pilate felt an unshakable fear crawl up his spine as he waited for My answer, which he knew would come eventually. The fear crawled up his spine like leeches clinging to him in order to suck the very life from him. Poor Pilate, he was just a pawn. The battle raging around him began thousands of years before he was born. The battle of good and evil, dark and light—and this particular battle would not be over until the hour of My crucifixion. Even after that, the spiritual battle will continue to rage for two thousand years, but during that time, all one has to do is call upon Me, Jesus, the Messiah. I will crush the serpent's head today and forever.

"Do you refuse to speak to me?" Pilate resounded in what sounded more a command than a question. "Don't you realize I have the power to either free you or to crucify you?"

If I was a mere man, I would have trembled before him, but I knew that all power had been given to Me and that I could use it or restrain it or give it to anyone I pleased. Absolute power belonged and always will belong to *Yahuweh*. I finally answered Pilate, breaking the heavy silence with words he could not understand, "You have no power over Me, except that it has been given to you from My Father. He who hands Me over to you is guilty of a greater sin."

I said this, for truly My people should have recognized Me as their Messiah instead of crucifying Me, but I knew before the foundation of the world this would be the path of My destiny; therefore, the prophets made mention of Me for thousands of years before this day in the Old Testament, the *Tanakh*.

Pilate *wanted* to let Me go, but He felt his hands were tied by an invisible thread—the scarlet thread of redemption that belonged to My Father only. It had to be so. The thread had been woven throughout history and would continue to be woven today until the end of the age.

Pilate pleaded with the Jewish leaders, but they answered back aggressively, "If you let this Man go, you are no friend of Caesar. Anyone who claims to be a king opposes Caesar!"

The shouts were relentless. Pilate brought Me out and sat down on the judge's seat at the Pavement, *Gabbatha*. It was between six and seven in the morning. Once more, Pilate presented Me before My People, "Here is your king!"

"Take Him away!" they shouted! "Crucify Him!"

Ugly, isn't it? The dark depth of a human heart?

All of Creation is lovely. The plants, trees, animals; the sun, moon, stars; the atmosphere that surrounds the Earth; the rain, snow, wind; the ocean depths, the mountain heights, but a human heart, who can know it?

"Shall I crucify your king?" Pilate asked.

"We have no king but Caesar!" My people answered.

Solemnly, with great trepidation, head hung low, eyes cast to the ground, Pilate handed Me over to be crucified. They eyes of the Jewish leaders were like hollow, vacant tombs, black holes of death with snakes writhing in momentary victory as the sentence was uttered. The demons, those of their father the devil, passed in and out of them. I could see them and hear them, clicking their teeth with cries of victory. Perhaps the sound, if I could describe it so you could understand, would sounds something like the gnashing of teeth.

But I was no longer thinking of the demons, the rabbis and the teachers. I was not thinking of Pilate, nor his wife, anymore. I was thinking of My beloved disciple, John. I was thinking of Mary of Bethany. I was thinking of Mary Magdalene and My mother, Mary. I was thinking of them huddled together outside Pavement—scared—shivering, murmuring among themselves, trying to comfort each other with very little success.

174

Of course, My mother would be attempting to comfort the others, even though she was suffering the most. She would recite stories of my youth. She would whisper words, such as... special, unique, full of words of wisdom, profound for My age. She would describe how she felt when she was pregnant with Me, a divine conception, and how she knew I would have to suffer one day.

She would be telling them these things to give them hope.

My beloved ones wanted to put their trust in her eyes. To rest in her words. They wanted to believe there was something greater going on in the midst of this dark hour. Although they did not understand, they loved Me to the end. They would follow as close to Me as they possibly could while I make My way up the Via Dolorosa. They would stand as close to Me as possible at Golgatha. I longed to comfort them, and soon My Spirit would comfort them, but for now, they had to trust in the love that I had lavished on them over the past years.

I was thinking how devious a human heart can be, but also how precious a human heart can be—one that is soft, loving and pliable. I was thinking how a tender heart can be a vessel for My Spirit to pour through, much like Myself, for I was a tender shoot.

"I had grown up like a tender shoot in Israel.
I grew like a root out of a dry and parched ground.
I had no beauty or majesty that made Me attractive to people.
Nothing in My appearance made people desire Me.
I was despised and rejected. I was and am a Man of suffering.
I am familiar with grief." Isaiah 53:2

I was now being led out of Gabbatha. The people who had wanted Me to be crucified could not look at My face anymore, as I passed among them. My face was too bloody and beaten. It was too grotesque. I, Jesus, am the face of *Yahuweh*. Their sins had marred My face, and yet if they would look at Me, they would see the love in My heart which shines through My eyes, even now. My heart beat with love for My people this day. As many who would receive Me, I would give them the right to be a son or daughter of God.

I was thinking of my tender ones, as I was thinking of you and am thinking of you now... Do not harden your heart when the road is rocky and the path that leads to eternal life is long. Look at Me, your Savior. My heart will beat for you and pump the very blood of My life into your tender heart. When your heart is pleading, silently weeping, think of Me, for I am thinking of you.

"I will save your tears in My bottle. I will write them in My book."
Psalm 56:8

It is for your tears pouring from your soft heart, that the tender heart of the Lamb of *Yahuweh* will die today; for I was thinking of you, as I am thinking of you now...

Let not your heart be troubled. Neither let it be afraid.

Take courage.

Setting...
Carrying the cross

Matthew 27
John 23

It was nearing the ninth hour of the morning as the soldiers stripped the purple robe from my body replaced it with My humble clothes. In order not to wince, they had to disassociate themselves from the wretched smell of My blood and sweat that clung to the "royal" robe. Of course, they had been desensitized over the years of their service to the Roman Government, but there was *something* about My robes, My clothes, that made the guards particularly uneasy. They quickly suppressed any misgivings they had. If they did not carry out Pilate's orders, they would themselves be in danger of being scourged.

The soldier who had the "honor" of removing my crown was pierced by the thorns as he jerked it from My skull. The thorns tore into his own wrists, and the blood squirted from his arms. He threw the crown wildly on the ground, kicked it deliberately, to get it as far away from him as he could. As his own blood ran down his arms, he witnessed the blood running down My skull from where the thorns had pierced Me. This site penetrated into his deepest soul.

"This is pure madness," he thought. What could this man have done to deserve this punishment? The thought only lasted a fleeting second. He knew he had to snap back into obedience, but before he could, he literally froze. He remembered a story he had been told by one of his comrades about a centurion from Capernaum.

A centurion would never speak candidly with someone like him, a common soldier. A centurion was a leader with a great amount of responsibility in the Roman Legion Army.

The soldier remembered that the centurion's servant was very ill. In fact, he was paralyzed, lying in intense suffering. The centurion had heard of Jesus, who could heal the sick and raise the dead. He had heard that this Jesus had raised Lazarus from the dead.

Although the Centurion was not of the Jewish faith, he sought out this Rabbi Jesus. He was the captain of the troop quartered in Capernaum, in the service of Herod Antipas. He was not a "proselyte of righteousness." He knew he was "unfit" to invite a Jewish Rabbi under his roof. This is why he searched the dusty streets in the shadows that evening to find Jesus, the story goes. It only so happened, this Jesus was nearby his house the night of his inquiry.

As the other soldiers continued to strip My robe in order to put My common clothes, soiled and torn, back on Me, the soldier with the blood running down his wrists, continued to be deeply involved in his inner struggle as he recalled more of the Centurion's story.

The Centurion heard that Jesus was walking toward his house. When he realized that Jesus had asked to come to his house to heal his servant, the Centurion sent friends out to Jesus, who replied with the Centurion's words, "No, I am not fit that You should come to my home, neither is my home fit for You. Just say the word, and he will be healed. For I, too, am a man set under authority, with soldiers under me; and I say to one, 'Go,' and he goes; and to another, 'come,' and he comes; and to my servant, 'do this,' and he does it."

While the Centurion's servants were speaking, Jesus healed the Centurion's servant.

As a lightning bolt of truth, this profound memory struck the soldier, and in a split-second, he realized the One standing before him had the power over life and death.

I, too remembered the healing and the Centurion's faith. I marveled at this man's faith in Me for...

"I had not found a faith so great in all of Israel." Matthew 8:10

Perhaps this soldier would share the same faith today.

"Look at Me," I whispered in My spirit. "Stop. Look at Me."

178

As an eternal drop of sunlight in the middle of a dark night, he brought his gaze to Mine. He found in an instant, an everlasting pool of pure love. In that second, he knew Me, as I knew him. Without anyone knowing what had just transpired, he was forever sealed into My plan of redemption. He bowed to Me in his heart, then stood up straight and took a deep breath.

With great distress, he joined the ranks as they brought Me to the entrance of the Via Dolorosa, just as he had to do. I did not blame him. He was now mine. If a person will look into My eyes and bow to Me with a humble heart, I will write their name in My book of life. They may be living under a harsh rule of a government, one which does not honor Me or in a culture where saying My name is taboo, but I will know them. In one look of humility that comes from their heart, they will be Mine forever.

Oh, if only the leaders of the synagogue could be like the Centurion, whose faith is so great that without the knowledge of even one word in the *Torah,* he has been written in My book of life, and secured his seat in heaven, much like the woman, who had been bleeding for 12 years, who touched My garment and was instantly made whole.

About three hours had passed since I had first stood before Pilate at six o'clock in the morning, but it felt to Me like eons of hours had passed. When one is suffering, it seems as if time stands still.

As the soldiers lifted the crossbeam onto My back, I could feel the weight of all the souls who ever were and were now and ever will be—heaved onto My shoulders. If only the weight I felt was merely the weight of the cross, I could have borne it more easily, but it was the sin of all of humanity—past, present and future—which bore down upon My weakened, bruised body, searing in pain.

Of course, I was carrying you on my shoulders, as well, because I was thinking of you, as I am thinking of you now...

I began My melancholy journey, one foot in front of the other, up the long road to the place of the skull, Golgotha, I carried the crossbeam from the last Gate which led from the Suburb. I walked by the Grotto of Jeremiah, the ancient place of stoning. I thought of how often My prophets have been stoned to death.

As I struggled along with a load much heavier than any human could imagine, I faltered and fell. It was apparent to the soldiers that My body was too weak now to last much longer. The soldier that had removed My crown of thorns, the one who had the change of heart, saw Simon, a man from Cyrene, standing in the crowd. Simon was a rugged man with broad, strong shoulders. The soldier abruptly ordered Simon to help Me.

Simon startled, that he was called out of the crowd, reluctantly stepped onto the road as he was ordered. Fearful of the Roman soldiers, he would, of course, do whatever they commanded.

He looked at Me tenderly, "Why was this sensitive Man carrying such a cross? Why was He ordered to be crucified?"

As the soldiers lifted the cross off My shoulders, the weight remained on Me. No one could see what I was bearing; the weight of the sins of the world was Mine alone to bear. Mine, alone.

Simon, however, carried his own cross as he shared in My suffering. It was his cross to bear, his purpose in life to help Me carry My cross. He knew it was not just a piece of wood he was ordered to carry. He could feel his family, his mother, his father, his wife, his children, his sisters and his brothers on his shoulders. He did not understand, but he could sense their lives were hanging in the balance, somehow depending on this moment.

Simon felt numerous conflicting emotions as he struggled up the hill with the crowd staring at him. He was not a criminal, but then again, neither was I. He could feel the goodness in Me. While he walked beside Me, I was thinking of him. I was weeping in My heart for each face, each heart, each servant of Mine who would ever help Me carry the cross — those who would deny themselves, take up their own crosses and follow Me.

I wept for the pain their sacrifice would cause them. I rejoiced with the glory they would share with Me at the end of the long road of suffering.

I was thinking of you, as you come along side Me. I know the way is arduous. Don't turn back. It is for the joy set before Me, that I endure the cross. It is for the joy of knowing you and of you knowing Me. Many will never understand the way of the cross. It is foolishness to those who are perishing, but to those who receive Me it is the power of God.

Wide is the door that leads to destruction, and *many* there will be who find it. Narrow is the way to eternal life, and few there will be who find it. Most will never understand why I had to die, but those who *know* they need a Savior will understand.

Nothing is balanced or moderate about My zeal for My people. It is perfectly imbalanced. I did it all for you. I became sin so that you become righteous. From this day forward, if you try to establish your righteousness or rely on your good works and rules to get you into heaven, you will be denying the perfect blood sacrifice of God. He who rejects Me, I will reject before My Father in heaven. He who accepts Me, I will accept into the kingdom of God.

I could feel the wrath of My Father in heaven mounting as the thick, grey clouds blew and covered Jerusalem – the wrath of the righteous God who requires justice.

Usually, in Rome, an interval of two days intervened between a sentence of execution and the actual execution, but this, of course, was not a normal execution.

Mourners gathered as I passed. Many followed Me. A large number of women and children were wailing for Me. I could hear their cries as I would hear the cries of My people throughout centuries to come. I turned and said to them,

"Daughters of Jerusalem, do not weep for Me;
Weep for yourselves and for your children,
For the time will come when you will say,
'Blessed are the childless women, the wombs that never bore
And the breasts that never nursed a baby.
They will say to the mountains, 'fall on us!' and to the hills, 'cover us!'
For if men do these things when the tree is green,
What will they do when it is dry." Luke 23:28-29

I said this to them because I knew destruction would come upon My people and the temple at Jerusalem after My death and resurrection.

Over time, women and children would often weep as their leaders would make unwise decisions and bring destruction upon their cultures and countries. I weep for them, as I weep for you now, when your sons and daughters go off to war and fight battles to keep your countries safe. Alas, there will always be war, until the time of this earth is over. One day, there will be one thousand years of peace on earth, and then, a new heaven and new earth, when the lion will lie down with the lamb.

I was thinking of you, when the leaders of your government, church, or family make corrupt decisions, and you are left homeless and penniless with children to care for.

Remember, I have a created a new home for you—an eternal home.

"Let not your heart be troubled; you believe in God,
Believe also in Me. In My Father's house are many mansions;
If it were not so, I would have told you.
I go to prepare a place for you. And if I go and prepare a place for you,
I will come again and receive you to Myself; that where I am,
There you may be also. And where I go you know, and the way you know."
John 14:1-4

I was thinking of you, just as I am thinking of you now...

Setting...
At the cross—Golgatha

Mark 15:22-31

After we passed gardens and tombs along the highway, we reached the gate just outside of Golgotha, near Jerusalem. Four centurions walked in formation around Simon and Me as he struggled to carry the cross up the last few steps to Golgotha. Two criminals in our procession each carried their own crossbeams on their shoulders.

A large crowd had gathered on the way as we made our hideous procession through the business quarter. The shops, bazaars and markets were closed due to the day of the Feast. As I moved slowly, painfully, on My way to My execution, people came out to see Me, and were humbled by the sight of this man, who called himself King of the Jews.

They pitied Me. I could hear it in their sighs. Some mocked Me. I appeared much like a worn-out homeless beggar who had been beaten in an alley and left to die. A poor, sad, tired face was what they saw. But, the pity should be for them, for I knew what Jerusalem would go through after My death.

I thought again how I had told the Pharisees and Sadducees,
"The kingdom of God will be taken away from you
And given to a people who will produce its fruit.
Anyone who falls on this stone will be broken to pieces,
Anyone on whom it falls, will be crushed." Luke 20:18
The Jewish leaders asked from where I got My authority.

I answered, *"Destroy this temple and in three days I will raise it up."*

They said, "It took forty-six years to build this temple!"

They did not understand that I was speaking of My body when I am raised from the dead. True worship from this day on, will be only in the Temple of Me, Jesus, the righteous Messiah.

As I looked like a slaughtered lamb proceeding towards Golgotha, enduring the mocking insults being hurled at Me, the hosannas of the week before echoed in my ear once again, when the multitude were singing, "Hosanna, Glory to God in the highest!" My triumphal entry, such a contrast to today's events, reminded Me that people are often swayed by the masses, and one should never give into peer pressure. Only do the will of God.

"For do I now persuade men, or God? Or do I seek to please men?
For if I yet pleased men, I should not be the servant of Christ."
Galatians 1:10

If I had relished in the praises of the people, it would have been harder for Me to bear their insults today. I had, instead, accepted their praise but not internalized it. As they laid the palm branches at My feet, a symbol of triumph and victory, I was thinking of you as I am thinking of you now...

I was thinking of the day when you might be praised and lifted up by a multitude, just to be crucified a week later by the same crowd. Do not lose heart. Ride on a colt with Me, in humility. Keep humble when you have the praise of people, because people can turn on you. Keep your eyes on your Father in heaven, for He dwells with the humble of heart.

When you are struggling up your own Via Dolorosa one day, carrying your own cross, I will be walking alongside you. I will be as Simone. I will help you carry your cross.

The crowd who cried, "Hosanna!" last week, is the same crowd who shouted, "Crucify Him!" this morning. I reflected on the fig tree, which symbolizes Israel, that bore no fruit as I wept.

"Jerusalem, Jerusalem, who kills the prophets
And stones those who are sent to her...
For I say to you, from now on you will not see Me until you say,
'Blessed is He who comes in the name of the Lord!'" Matthew 23:37-39

One day, not too far off from now, there will be another kind of weeping and wailing in Jerusalem. They will see Me, the One whom they have pierced, and they will mourn for Me as one mourns for an only child, and grieve bitterly for him as one grieves for a firstborn son when...

"I will pour out on the house of David and on the inhabitants of Jerusalem,
The Spirit of Grace and of supplication,
so that they will look on Me whom they have pierced;

And they will mourn for Him, as one mourns for an only son, and
They will weep bitterly over Him like the bitter weeping over firstborn."
Zechariah 12:10

When I come in the clouds in My second coming, they will say, "Blessed is He who comes in the name of the Lord."

Zechariah prophesied of Me,

"In that day His feet will stand on the Mount of Olives,
Which is in front of Jerusalem on the East;
And the Mount of Olives will be split in its middle from east to west
By a very large valley, so that half of the mountain will move toward
The north and the other half toward the South."
Zechariah 14:4

We now passed through the gate to enter Golgotha, which means skull, a very strange, dreary place, a few minutes from the high road. The rocky plateau is a skull-like formation with a sunken, hollow place beneath it, as if the skulls of a jaw are opened. This place seemed fitting for the horrific event of crucifixion. Humans throughout thousands of years will invent torturous apparatuses and methods in which to harm and to kill one another. Crucifixion, originated by the Assyrians and Babylonians, later brought to the Romans by the Phoenicians is one of the most brutal and shameful forms of death. The Romans would use it today and will continue to use it for hundreds of years after My death to disgrace soldiers, Christians and foreigners.

As I watched Simon bring the crossbeam to the large post laying on the ground, I was not thinking of the suffering that I would continue to endure. I was thinking of the suffering My people would endure when they have realized they crucified their own Messiah. I was thinking of the suffering the soldiers would endure when they realized they have crucified the Son of God.

I am thinking of the suffering you may endure one day when you walk away from Me, cursing the very blessing I bring. Come back to Me. Take heart. I break the curse, once and forever.

One day, there will be no more curse... In New Jerusalem, the water of life, the living waters, clear as crystal will flow from the throne of the Lamb. On either side of the river will be a tree of life, which bears twelve fruits every month. The leaves will be for the healing of the nations. And there shall be no more crying, no more sickness, no more death, no curse. The throne of *Yahuweh* and of the Lamb, shall be in the midst. His servants shall see His face and His name shall be on their foreheads. There will be no night there. *Revelation 22*

The glory of *Yahuweh* shown in My eyes as they wrangled Me to the cross. If anyone here could see past My decrepit body, into My soul, they would see eternity shining brighter than the sun. The glory of God was upon Me—as I became the curse to break the curse for all time.

As it is written about Me,

> *"Christ redeemed us from the curse of the law, having become a curse*
> *For us; for it is written in Deuteronomy 21:23, 'Cursed is every one*
> *That hangs on a tree.' Cursed is everyone who hung on a cross."*
> *Galatians 3:13*

Simon lifted the crossbeam off of his weary shoulders, and lowered it down to the dirt. I was then pushed down violently onto of the rugged piece of wood.

Behold the Lamb of God who takes away the sins of the world. Behold the Lamb of God who takes away your sins.

> *"I separate your sins as far as the East is from the West*
> *And remember them no more." Psalm 103:12*

I was thinking of you, years from now, when you need a blessing to break your curse...

I am that Blessing.

A soldier brought forth a board, on which to write gypsum letters. It was a custom to hang the board above the one crucified as to identify what they had done. In My case, they wrote in Greek, Hebrew and Latin —"KING OF THE JEWS."

The crowd went wild... "Ha! Ha! You were going to destroy the temple and rebuild it in three days! Save yourself! Come down from that cross, you King of the Jews!"

"He saved others, but He cannot save himself," the chief priests mocked Me.

"Let this Christ, the King of Israel, now come down from the cross, so we may see and believe!" They roared with laughter.

I come as a Lamb today. I will be nailed to this cross today. Tomorrow, I will come as a Lion. If is a fearful thing to fall into the hands of a living God. I am the Alpha, the Omega, the Beginning and the End. My kingdom is not of this earth and My kingdom shall have no end.

The sky darkened even more now. The crowd hushed. Many people grew fearful.

I could have splintered the cross into a million pieces with one word from My mouth. I could have opened up the earth in a great earthquake and swallowed each person here.

No. I would not.

Years ago, the prophet Elijah trembled, hiding in the cave, after he challenged the eight hundred false prophets of Baal. He won the challenge, but afterward, alone and afraid, in a quiet cave, he really got to *know* Me.

"And, behold, the Lord passed by,
And a great and strong wind rent the mountains,
And brake in pieces the rocks before the Lord;
But the Lord was not in the wind: and after the wind an earthquake;
But the Lord was not in the earthquake: and after the earthquake a fire;
But the Lord was not in the fire: and after the fire a still small voice..."
1 Kings 19:11-12

My greatest glory would be accomplished today on this cross. The cross is the still small voice of God. My willingness to die for all of humanity, would make an open spoil over the enemy for all time. Many gods will come forth and say, "Worship Me! Follow Me!" But only *one* God will die for you—*Yahuweh.*

You will know My voice, the voice of the Good Shepherd. The blood I shed will shake the foundations of lies and false religion and My water will pour out a stream of life to give nourishment to the world. The depth of My love for you is deeper than hell and more expansive than the universe.

As the criminals next to Me were being nailed to their crosses, the pounding filled the air with an ominous feeling, a tangible sinking feeling of dread.

I remained focused on you. You are My prize. I was fresh and full of vigor at the beginning of My ministry, but in a few moments, I will be nailed to a cross. At the beginning of your ministry you will be full of enthusiasm, yet after years of labor, toil and persecutions, you may become weary. When you are persecuted, taken advantage of, gossiped about, and falsely accused, and nailed to a cross prepared for you by the false leaders, the crowd, I am with you.

For I was thinking of you, as I am thinking of you now...

Setting...
At the cross—Golgatha

Luke 23:32-37

The executioner loomed over Me, holding the seven-inch long, iron nails. I lay beneath him much like a lamb being held down before he is slaughtered. With the angle in which I was viewing him, he appeared to be nine feet tall, much like a demonic principality, who was once an esteemed angel in My heavenly host. The black clouds above, also, cast an eerie gloom over him. The shapes in the clouds appeared to Me like sinister serpents with hissing tongues, winged and fanged, snickering.

The air became menacing with an overwhelming stench of something rancid. When sin abounds, the atmosphere is even contaminated by the sin. The sin rises to the nostrils of My Father with a putrid, acrid odor, in contrast to the prayers of saints which rise to Him like sweet smelling incense.

The foreboding hour of darkness had come, and satan would take full advantage of this short time to gloat over the Son of God. I was stretched out, flat on My back. I did not resist or shout, nor did I cry out when the executioner bent over and began to drive the nails deep into My flesh.

He now pounded the first nail between the small bones on My wrist. He hammered, until the nail pierced through to the rugged wood of the cross.

The pounding of the nails into My flesh appeared to be a tragedy, but it was in fact the resounding beat of the foundation being constructed of the new Temple. The Temple, My body, was being prepared—the eternal Temple of God built on the Cornerstone, Me, and My sacrifice for you.

"The stone which the builders rejected has become the chief corner stone."
Psalm 118:22

For you, for you... I recited to Myself as the nails pounded into the tender soft tissue of My feet, ripping through My muscles, My sinews, My veins. The pounding seemed to last an eternity. With searing pain shooting through My body that was beyond comprehension, I wanted to die now. I did not want to be hung on the cross and endure the excruciating torture of hanging by My wounded wrists and mutilated feet until I suffocated.

But I knew I had to complete what I had begun. The curse of humanity would be broken only by My sacrifice on the cross. The hands which once fed the five thousand, along with the women and the children, were now were pinned to a degrading, disgusting execution stake. My hands in My future glory will nourish welcome My sons and daughters into heaven. I had to focus on the glory set before Me.

As My heel was crushing the head of the serpent for all time, both of My feet were being pierced with a huge nail—the same feet that walked throughout the countrysides of Galilee to heal the sick and raise the dead—the same feet Mary of Magdalene had poured oil over and washed with her hair—the same feet that would stand in a resurrected form only three days from now—the same feet which would command the reverence of the whole world years from now on the Mount of Olives—one nail driven near both heels. Perhaps it was satan's way of adding an additional injury to insult in order to fulfill the scriptures' prophecy, *"The serpent will bruise his heel."*

What was being carried out was a fulfillment of My Father's promise to Eve and all of her children,

"The seed of a woman will crush the serpent's head,
While the serpent will bruise his heel." Genesis 3:15

I had been written into the plan from the beginning of all time. Even in the curse of the Garden after the fall of Adam and Eve, which brought sin into the world, there was a promised blessing—Me, Jesus, the Righteous Messiah.

The serpent, of course, was inhabited by satan, who was Lucifer, My chief musician and once prized angel. He desired to be worshipped like God so he had to be cast out of heaven, along with one-third of My angels, who are now demons. Thus, satan seeks people to worship him as he roams the earth like a tainted lion, seeking whomever he can devour. He appears as an angel of light. He offers lies that are so tasty-looking, he will deceive many. But he and his fallen angels know their time is short. One day they will be cast into the abyss forever.

190

My work on the cross today is the crowning glory of My Kingship. All power has been given to Me as I make an open spoil over the enemy.

I thought about the soldier that held the nail as it was being pounded near my heel. What a strange task for a man to perform—to nail another man to a cross. Did this soldier think about this very act when he was a boy? Did he hope to grow up and be a murderer? Did he want to be a centurion in the Roman army? Or did he want to be a carpenter or a winemaker? What if he wanted to be an artist?

How could he stand to see the blood squirting from my ankle? How could he keep the nail steady as the other soldier performed the forceful blows that drove it through My flesh? If his hand shook, the nail might not pierce the proper place, thus breaking my bones. My bones were not to be broken today. It was prophesied that even if my bones were to fall out of joint, none would be broken, just as the Passover lambs bones were not to be broken.

For these things were done that the Scripture should be fulfilled,
"Not one of His bones shall be broken." John 19:36

What if the one using the hammer missed the nail and hit the soldier instead? Had they practiced this many times? I thought about these men as they nailed my feet to the Latin-shaped cross. Would they drink tonight and celebrate the successful crucifixion? Would they remember Me when they slept tonight on their beds? Would they toss and turn with remorse and guilt?

I was thinking of them, as I was thinking of you, as I am thinking of you now... Did you sin in a manner where only a nail driven into a Savior on a cross could redeem you? No one else has to know, but I know. I am thinking of you—as I lie here fastened to a cross, a hideous spectacle, My chest heaving, My body laboring to stay alive a little while longer until it is finished. Every muscle in my body aches. Every nerve, every fiber is groaning with pain and anguish.

When you face your most hidden sin in—the one you have buried deep in your heart, you will know you have a Savior who hung on the cross and stayed on the cross just for you. I could have torn the nails from My flesh. I could have leapt into the crowd and said, "Ah ha! I am King. Worship Me now!" But because My Father required a perfect blood sacrifice, for your sake, I hung on—

I stayed so that you could come to Me one day. Pour out your heart to Me. Come under the blood and find redemption. My dream was for you

191

to live, and truly be the person you were created to be, without guilt, sin, fear, doubt, or shame.

The boyhood of these soldiers was quite far from their minds, but to Me they were still boys. I knew they would suffer from what they had just done. How could they not? A man hurting a man who has done nothing wrong? A person punishing an innocent person? The nail they drove into my flesh would come back to pierce their very own hearts.

The sky was pitch black now. People's faces were covered with uneasiness and dread as they noticed the darkened sky. The clouds were so thick, it was if it was midnight in mid-afternoon. The sun hid its face for these hours as My Father in heaven had commanded. It will be dark for some time as this present madness continues. Death by crucifixion can take six hours or up to four days. I did not think I could go through another second of this pain.

As the soldiers lifted up the cross on which My body was attached, to place Me between the two criminals, they did not know they were fulfilling prophetic scripture.

"Just as Moses lifted up the snake in the wilderness,
So the Son of Man must be lifted up, that everyone who believes
In Him may have eternal life...." John 3:14

Moses lifted up the brass snake I had told him to make, which will become a symbol of healing in the medical field, the children of Israel were healed of the plague. And now, as I am lifted up, I will draw all people to Myself, heal their diseases and save them from eternal damnation.

"Then the LORD said to Moses, 'Make a fiery serpent,
And set it on a standard; and it shall come about,
That everyone who is bitten, when he looks at it, he will live.'
And Moses made a bronze serpent and set it on the standard;
And it came about, that if a serpent bit any man,
When he looked to the bronze serpent, he lived." Numbers 21:8-9

To some people, this seemed illogical. Why would God want the people to look at a statue of a bronze serpent lifted up on a pole to be healed?

The questions will be the same with My crucifixion, "Why would I need a Savior? Someone who lived and died thousands of years ago? Some man, who called Himself, Jesus, who died on a cross? Why is it important to me?"

"For it pleased the Father that in Me should ALL fullness dwell;
And, having made peace through the blood of his cross,
I, Jesus, reconcile all things unto Myself;
Whether they be things in Earth or things in heaven." Colossians 1:19-20
"I cancel out the certificate of debt consisting
Of decrees against you, which are hostile to you;
I take them out of the way, nail them to the cross—
When I had disarmed the rulers and authorities,
Making a public display of them, by My death and resurrection."
Colossians 1:14-15 (Paraphrased)

As the vertical wooden post of the cross was being pounded into the ground, My body jerked and jolted in pain. I looked up to heaven and cried,

"Father, forgive them, for they know not what they are doing."

Some people watching still sneered and jested among themselves, "He saved others, but He cannot save himself."

I knew fear, sin and doubt in their hearts. The ugliness of the cross is the culmination of the ugliness of sin placed upon it. Upon the cross lay the sins of the world. When other gods vie for attention, and they will—the cross will be the pivotal point of illumination. Any god may live for people. But only *one* God will die. To take the place of another is the greatest expression of friendship and of love.

As physically excruciating it is to be hung on the branches of an olive tree with your limbs pierced, the humiliation is equally brutal. I had been stripped naked again. Not even a thin garment to shield Me from the disgrace.

As the soldiers cast lots for my robes, I grieved most as they bet on my inner garment, the one that is woven in one piece. I did not grieve that I was naked. Even stripped to the bone—No, it was for you that I grieved, for I was thinking of you, as I am thinking of you now...

For the times when you would be humiliated, publicly or privately by your own spouse when he betrays you or when a group casts lots for your very own person, and you will be subject to them as a slave. Or when a women is sold to the highest bidder as a wife or becomes a servant among her relatives. Or worse than that, when a young girl is sold to an older neighbor in exchange for a cow.

It is when you feel naked and alone, you need to know you have the right to be covered. It is when you feel violated, you need to know that, even though someone can hurt your body, there is no one who can rob your soul. I was thinking of your soul, as I am thinking of you now. I am the protector of your soul.

Human decency is more important than human torture or even death. Even a criminal who deserves to die warrants a decent death. In My delicate human condition, I watched them cast lots right at my feet, and I grieved for those that would be found naked one day, against their will, tortured and humiliated beyond recognition. It is why I, with obedience entered into the humiliation, and it is why I remain on the degrading cross. I had already made My decision, and there was no turning back.

As the soldiers were casting lots over My garments, My loved ones wanted to rush in and cast their lot so that they could save My garments and preserve them as a memory of Me, but the lots had to be cast to fulfill the prophecy,

"They divided My garments among them and cast lots for my clothing."

Psalm 22:16

I thought of My mother in the distance and the women who had stood by Me. I knew they could not bear the sight of Me at this point, but they attempted to look bravely on. My mother would be certainly numb with anguish. I prayed for the Angel of the Lord to strengthen her. The one who had strengthened Me in the Garden of Gethsemane. I thought of her eyes, so full of love. Each time she looked at Me as a child, I felt a warm eternal embrace. I prayed she would feel the same embrace now as her Son hung bleeding and dying on a cross.

The vessel through which I had chosen to enter the Earth was as pure as pure could be. My mother, Mary, would love me to the end. I knew she would take My place if I would let her. I knew it as much as I know the beginning from the end.

I was the author and finisher of her faith, but ironically, she had possessed the womb from which I had come. How great a love is a good mother. I wished for her sake I did not have to finish this business of salvation, but I also knew for her sake I knew I must, for even My mother needed a Savior.

All have sinned and come short of the glory of God.

I saw her trembling, her lip quivering as she bravely stood strong for Me. She would not cower or shrink back. No. Even though she did not understand the whole picture, she knew that I was the beloved Son of My Father in heaven and that I walked a unique path on this Earth.

The women braced themselves near her. They tried to hold her up, but she, in fact, was holding them up. These beloved few kept close with Me, having stayed up all night, crying with despair. They felt helpless. What could they do to fight against the Roman Government? They had walked up the hill close behind Me, as did My dear disciple, John.

I looked at My mother's sad, long face—her eyes pleading for answers, for some sense of relief. I witnessed John's precious face peering up at Me with eternal love, but full of questions. I whispered to her and to John in a hoarse breath...

"Dear woman, here is your son."

And I said to him,

"Here is your mother."

He would take care of her the rest of her life.

They had to strip Me so when your private thoughts are exposed to the vicious public by some ignorant person's revenge, and you feel you have been stripped bare before a ruthless crowd, you will know that your Savior experienced the same degradation. Your human decency is safe with Me. In the Temple of My body, your mind, your heart, your body, and your soul are covered in white linen from heaven.

You are safe with Me now. You are safe with Me always. I will always defend you with the cost of My own life.

My chest is heaving now. To take in the smallest amount of air into my lungs, I must push up on my nail-bound feet. My body is involuntarily doing this in order to stay alive. I am dehydrated, tortured beyond repair. My shoulders are out of joint...

It won't last much longer. Be of good cheer, I told Myself over and over, as I tell you now—I have overcome the world.

I was thinking of you, as I am thinking of you now...

Setting…
Gogaltha—The Thieves

John 19:23-24

The blackening sky deemed an ominous covering. The people who were unwavering just hours ago in their decision I should be condemned to die, now cowered under the increasing oppression of the atmosphere. The masses grew restless, but instead of moving as a mob, they began prodding each other much like cattle panicking when a storm is pending, frantically colliding with one another pushing their way to shelter.

What if this was *truly* the Son of God? The sheer density of the dark clouds conveyed the impression of thick, heavy mud weighing heavily on *their* shoulders. The thick, murky air oozed into their ears, their eyes, even into their mouths. The once confident cries, of "Crucify Him!" now felt more like hoarse whispers, muddled with fear, much like a cry in a nightmare, when one opens their mouth to scream, but no sound is heard.

This is the tone of My final hour before My death. Due to multifactorial pathology, the after-effects of compulsory scourging and maiming, hemorrhage and dehydration, My body is in severe shock.

With each labored breath, I heaved up and down on the nails that bore into My flesh. I felt as if I was being suffocated, asphyxiated—strangled by the weight of My very own body. The body I inhabited in order to walk among My people of Israel—My body, once a blessing to many—now a curse, hanging on a tree.

I was thinking of you, as I am thinking of you now… when a pernicious envelope closes in around you, when the enemies are hauntingly gruesome and you sense their wicked, evil presence—seemingly fenced in with no way out. When the enemy of your soul is pressing down on you with a heaviness on your chest, which makes you feel suffocated and paralyzed; this is the opposite of My Presence. My Presence is One of peace and will cause you to feel empowered, strengthened, confident and assured. I am the Light of the world. I am the same in the light and the darkness. I will illuminate your darkness. Call upon Me, Jesus. In My name, demons flee.

The two criminals on either side of me groaned as they were lifted up unto the stationary member of each of their crosses. They had not been scourged. Their faces were recognizable. Each had committed a common crime.

As I was being lifted up, with blood running everywhere from My hands, My feet, My face, My head, My back, My chest, one of the criminals jeered at Me, "Aren't you the Christ? Save yourself and us!"

I would have looked at them if My eyes were not so swollen from the beatings, and the pain was not shooting through My body as a lightning bolt, as I hung vertically, causing My weight to bear down on My wounds.

The irony of being a perfect Man crucified between two thieves was not too difficult for Me to bear. It was, in fact, the two thieves who faced their own conflict in being crucified next to Me. The bickering between people regarding who I am was a common theme as I walked the Earth. It is common now to these two thieves drawing conclusions about who I am—arguing even while they are dying on a cross, and even while I am in the midst of them, listening to their discourse.

I, of course, could see the hearts of these men. I knew why they were here. I knew why they were condemned to die today. They, however, did not know nor begin to understand why I am here. Would they believe Me if I told them I was nailed to a cross because of My great love I have for humanity? Of My great love I have for them?

The thief on My left hurled insults at Me, "If you are the Christ, save yourself and us!... "

How is it that he had the strength to speak at all?

The one on My right answered, rebuking the first one, "Do you not even fear God, since you are under the same sentence of condemnation? We indeed are suffering justly, for we are receiving what we deserve for our deeds, but this Man has done nothing wrong."

As they continued the bickering, I thought about the future and destiny of people from now on. There will always remain the same controversy based on My identity—whenever the name of Jesus is mentioned, until I come again, there will be the conflict of the two thieves.

Just as I am experiencing first-hand the squabbling, as they hurl their opinions to each other; even as I hang, bleeding and dying between them, millions of people throughout thousands of years will carry on the exact same debate. In churches and out of churches, in Christian cultures and non-Christian cultures, there will be the ongoing dialogue—*who* am I?

I, of course, will be in the middle of them, stretching out My hands daily for their sakes, and each dispute will be much like these two thieves—quarreling about the validity of My claim to be God. Even as they are condemned to death, for each person must die, like these two criminals, the opposing sides will be quibbling about Me, instead of facing their own judgement and certain execution.

So many people will miss the point—*Me*. Over and over and over they will miss the pivotal, crucial point of My mission on Earth—to die so that others may live. As I am lifted up in the middle of sinful humans, I cannot be forgotten or put aside. I cannot be discredited by anyone's opinion of Me. I stand forever, as God who became Man and poured out My life for all those who would receive Me. It doesn't matter to Me what any person thinks of Me; it matters to them.

I was thinking of each thief next to Me. I knew their thoughts, their actions. I knew when they got up and sat down. I knew when they decided to commit each crime and exactly what drove them to it. I even knew what they would choose at this critical moment.

Throughout generations, I will be the subject of countless conversations. As each conversation occurs, I will be in their midst—right there. I am right there now, as you speak of Me, wonder about Me, perhaps even make your own opinions of Me. My hands will still be stretched out for you, for I was thinking of you, as I am thinking of you now...

As one thief began to harden his heart, he held his head high defiant with pride, as painful as it was. It grieved Me so. I did not want him to be separate from Me. I wanted him to be in the kingdom of God with Me this very day—to join Me with My Father in heaven, but I could feel his heart turning to stone. One more chance I was giving him. One more chance, but much like a petrified piece of wood which becomes stone over time, this man's heart had become hard. Each time he had a chance to humble his heart and try to have better life, he had taken another step on the path to darkness.

Once his heart had been pliable, like clay. Something could be made from it. I thought of his heart when he was just a boy. As any boy, he had curiosity and wonder. He carefully formed a pile of mud into a lion that he could play with. One day, he got beat up by a cruel neighbor boy, and he remembers the day he took his clay lion, threw it onto the ground, it broke into pieces. He made the clay into a stone he could throw instead. This was his first turning point, which started him on a pathway to hatred and revenge, and later crime.

"I deserve to steal this bread," he muttered to himself as he took his first piece, "because it is a cruel world. If I don't feed myself, no one will."

I could hear his thoughts which led to the pattern which paved the path to his destruction. I loved him. I would have reached out my hands to him if I could, even my heart to him, but the pliable wood of a boy had become a putrid tomb.

His attitude was in such acute contrast to the criminal on my right. This one could not even look at Me. He only stared at the ground near My feet, where his shadow was cast. He felt he was not worthy to be crucified next to Me. He wished he could withdraw his shadow that dared to touch My feet.

Perhaps many times he had heard of Me, but he had kept on with his path of crime. Perhaps someone even tried to give him a slice of bread, but he felt unworthy to receive such a benevolent gift as he had so often stolen the same crumb for his own sake.

I saw his heart. Is it strange that in My final moments of life in a mortal body, I should be considering the thieves on either side of Me? The two thieves will reflect the two opposing opinions of Me throughout the rest of history. The two thieves' attitudes, one in arrogance, one in humility, warrant attention as these two attitudes will serve as an example of the choice given to each person from this day forward.

Who do men and women say that I am? Who do the thieves say I am? One shouts that I am a fraud while the other acknowledges Me as a King and begs for mercy. The thief on my right dared to whisper My name, "Jesus, remember me when You come in Your kingdom."

Who do you say that I am? This will be the recurring theme throughout generations. It is no mistake that My last interface with humans would be one of two very different sentiments, and that this interaction would be one with strangers and thieves. Anyone has the right to call upon Me and be saved, even to their last breath.

When I said to the one on my right,

"Truly I say to you, today you shall be with Me in paradise."
Luke 23:43

I exemplified for all times that anyone with the proper heart towards Me will have the right to enter the kingdom of God. One does not need to do any work other than to believe on Me. One does not have to be baptized or become a church member. One only has to believe that I am the Messiah, Jesus Christ, the Son of God, the Savior of the world.

"For God so loved the world, that he gave his only begotten Son,
That whosoever believes in Him should not perish,
But have everlasting life." John 3:16

You might think I am cruel, by not letting the thief on my left enter into paradise with Me, but this man had many, *many* chances throughout his life to believe in God. He *chose* not to believe. Even in his final hour, God had given him one last chance. God is gracious, full of mercy and kindness. He gives a person every chance to come to Him.

Just as the thieves had secured their fate, one to hell, the other one to heaven, each person must make a decision on their own. Just I had to bear My cross alone, each person must bear their cross alone, with one exception—I will be there. No one could do this for Me. I had created humankind; I must save them from themselves.

Throughout the rest of the history of the world, as the church age rises, there will be the same dialogue going on between two thieves. I will be continually stretched out between the two swords of opinion, whether they are real swords or a cold war. My death on the cross will be forever in the middle of the war.

As each thief speaks his or her mind, their opinions will burn like dry tinder in the flaming fire of My presence and become nothing but ashes in the Light of My word. My Truth will ultimately burn up the rhetoric. Only a choice counts. Believe who I am, or not.

Throughout crusades and religious wars, where one person kills another in My name, I will be in the middle—the One who is being slaughtered for their sakes all day long. Throughout fussing and fighting between religious organizations, I will be the common denominator—the only One who has the right to be worshipped. My arms will be continually open to receive anyone who stops, listens and with humility casts his or her eyes to the ground in My presence, just like the thief on My right.

201

Each sword that is thrust in My name must pierce through Me first, as it is now, for I am the true Temple. In Me is the fullness of *Yahuweh* forever. A church with no walls is My body. A church with no denomination is My body. A church with no doctrine but Me, My word, is My body. A church who welcomes everyone as guests to a wedding feast is My body. My body *is* the church, and I am the only One who needs to die for the sins of the world.

You should never be punished for your sins by another person. If someone comes to kill you in My name, then he or she is not in fellowship with Me, the living God. If someone comes with another doctrine to add to My death on the cross, then he or she is *not* coming in the name of the Lord.

There will be many horrific deeds done in My name throughout the rest of the history of the world, but these acts are much the same as the thieves fighting amongst themselves. I will always be separate. I will infinitely be the One lone Savior of the world. I am not an organization, not an entity. I am a person, a Deity—the Man/God who died alone to open a door through My body and My blood for anyone to come into My sanctuary and fellowship with Me in peace.

As I think of the words and swords which will continue years from now, as I hang on this rugged cross. Although My body is screaming in pain, I silently remain, steadfast, so that when you are crushed under the weight of someone's false doctrine, or you are caught in the middle of a denomination war, or at the point of someone's wicked religious sword—you will know that *I am He*—the One who is the First and the Last, the Alpha and Omega, the *Aleph* and *Tov*. What I started, I will finish—the beginning and the end, the author and the finisher of your faith.

I am the door to paradise and eternal peace. Just as I take the humble thief with Me this day to paradise, I will take you. I was thinking of you, just as I am thinking of you now. In all demonstration of religious zealotry throughout all time, the demonstration of My death on the cross is the pivotal point of faith. I am at the center. When you are in pain, afraid and alone, when you are at the point of death, call upon Me, and truly, you will be with Me this day in paradise. As I said,

"Where I go there are many mansions. Do not let your heart be troubled. Do not let it be afraid. Where I go I prepare a place for you."
John 14:2

I prepare this place for you today, just as I am moments away from the end of my life in human form. As I am at death's door, the Door is opening for you to be with Me in paradise forever.

I am thinking of you…

Setting...
Golgatha

Matthew 27:45-50

Darkness continued to cover the Earth until My death. Even the birds were confused and stopped chirping, thinking it was nighttime. I recalled the words of Amos, who prophesied, "Woe unto you who desire the day of the Lord. To what end is it for you? The day of the Lord is darkness, and not light. As if a man did flee from a lion, and a bear met him; or went into the house, leaned his hand on the wall, and a serpent bit him. Shalt not the day of the Lord be darkness, and not light? Even very dark with no brightness." *Amos 5:18-20*

Everyone noticed the ominous sky. An eclipse of the sun only happens when the moon is directly between the sun and the earth, blocking out its light. This day of My death there is a full moon, because it is Passover. The moon is on the far side of the Earth, far away from the sun, but regardless, this day the sun refused to shine. A supernatural eclipse of the sun took place for three hours. The three hours are symbolic of the three days I will lay in the tomb.

Death on a cross was most commonly precipitated by cardiac arrest, initiated by consequential loss of oxygen in the blood, severe pain, body blows and breaking of the large bones. The attending Roman guards could only leave the site after the victim had died, and were known to precipitate death by means of deliberate fracturing of the tibia, the larger bone of the leg between the knee and ankle, and/or the fibula, the smaller bone between the knee and the ankle. They also might spear stab wounds into the heart, or deliver sharp blows to the front of the chest, or even build a smoking fire at the foot of the cross to asphyxiate the victim faster.

I would have no bones broken, as it was prophesied, and with the black night of day, the soldiers were leery to approach Me at this point, let alone break My bones.

I could barely breath. My breath was labored and forced. My body shook violently from the pain and blood loss.

I am now suffering not only because I have been forsaken by those I came to save, not only because of the physical pain I am enduring, but because of the complete lack of light that I am experiencing. I had endured all of this in order to be My obedient to My Father, with whom I had walked closely with during My time on the Earth. The fellowship with My Father who gives every good gift and is perfect from above. His Presence is in Me and with Me as I fulfilled My ministry. Even as a young boy, I could feel His perfect love with Me at all times.

The rejection of My people and the physical suffering is nothing compared to the rejection I feel as the Presence of My Father withdraws from Me. Sin is dark and has no light in it. The Father does not dwell in sin or have any part with it. Sin is separate from God. As I bear the excessive and ominous burden of the sin of humanity, I bear it in human flesh... alone, alone—*alone*.

The Father did not send an angel to strengthen Me like He did in the Garden last night. He did not transfigure Me as He did on the Mount of Transfiguration. He did not shelter Me as He did when Herod's men raided Israel in order to kill all of the male babies when I was newly born. He did not hide Me in His Presence as he did when I walked away from the religious leaders who wanted to kill Me before it was My time to die.

I could not *feel* Him at all.

Out of My obedience to the Father, I would allow the complete wrath of a holy and righteous God to descend on Me.

My people of Israel had rejected Me. Those whom I had been raised with in my local synagogue had scorned Me, criticized Me and had finally condemned Me to death. The representatives of the temple, who proclaimed to be worshipping God, treated Me worse than a common criminal. Those who are ignorant often ridicule what they do not understand. The priests laughing nearby are the perfect example.

Eleven of My disciples had not understood Me even though they followed Me closely and were dearly devoted to me. They had deserted Me when I sweat drops of blood in the garden of decision. My right-hand man, Judas, had betrayed Me with a kiss. My beloved Peter cursed and swore he did not know Me as I was on My way to be incriminated for telling the truth.

The religious authorities accused Me before Annias, who later sent Me to Caiaphas, then to the Sanhedrin, who spit in My face, beat Me, and mocked Me. The Roman soldiers had used Me as a punching bag. The Sanhedrin did not go with Me into the Praetorium where I was condemned to die so they would not defile themselves before the Passover Feast.

The crowds of people, some of whom had followed Me for three and half years, chose Barabbas to be released rather than Me. Pilate advocated for My life, but ended up rejecting Me when he washed his hands, releasing himself of the responsibility pertaining to My case. Herod abandoned Me when he passed Me back to Pilate. Pilate relinquished himself to the people's wishes. The rejection continued as I was mockingly called, "King of the Jews." Even the thief on My left rejected Me.

All of this rejection I could bare, but the rejection from My Father in heaven at this hour of My death, after enduring the most humiliating and torturous of deaths, was more than I could bare.

"Eli, Eli, lena sabachthani? My God, My God, Why have You forsaken Me?"

I screamed this my very last bit of strength, fulfilling the prophecy in Psalm 22.

Here I was, nailed to the cross in a position that is impossible to maintain, where My knees are flexed at an approximately 45 degree angle, which forced My weight to bear on the muscles of My thighs. Every few minutes My thighs and calves would cramp severely. Any weight on My feet only worsened the pain in the areas where the nail was driven through.

When the strength of My muscles of My lower limbs tired, the weight of My body had to be transferred to My wrists, My arms, and My shoulders. The weight of the sin of humanity dislocated my shoulders, elbows, and wrists—each in a matter of minutes after being hung on the cross. My arms were now nine inches longer than before, and still they stretched out to receive you unto Myself.

For I was thinking of you, as I am thinking of you now...

As David prophesied, I was poured out like water.

After My wrists, elbows, and shoulders were dislocated, the weight of My body on My upper limbs caused traction forces on the pectoral muscles of My chest wall. The force caused My ribcage to be pulled upwards and outwards, in a most unnatural state.

My chest wall was permanently in a position of maximal respiratory expiration. In order to exhale, I was physiologically required to force My body upward. As I did this, it required Me to push down on the nails in My feet to raise My body, in order to allow My ribcage to move downwards and inwards. Twelve inches up. Twelve inches down. Up. Down. Up. Down. Up. Down, while My blood poured out of My hands, My feet, My back, My face, My head, all the while enduring the wrath of My Father.

This process of breathing caused excruciating pain. Excruciating is a word derived from crucifixion. Crucifixion is a medical catastrophe. The fact that an innocent Man was made to endure crucifixion is a calamity of all of humanity, one which needs to be examined.

You might say, "I don't have any guilt." I realize guilt will be an unpopular phrase in the twenty-first century. Nevertheless, I took your guilt on the cross and nailed it to Myself. As the six hours of the crucifixion wore on, I became less able to bear the weight in any part of My body. The fear of suffocating was terrifying, but with the pain in My shattered nerves in My wrists exploded with every slight movement, as I heaved Myself up.

Covered in blood, sweat and humiliation from being naked, as the leaders of the Jewish people, the crowds, the thief and the soldiers were continuing to jeer, swear and laugh at Me—I went inward. I had to find a place in Myself that would encourage Me to stay on this cross of suffering. I had to reflect on the Creation – My creation of humankind. I had to reflect on the beginning in order to finish.

I was the author and the finisher of the faith of the world. I had to remember why I created Adam and Eve in the first place. I desired fellowship with those who were made in My image. I created humans to have a heart and soul, to be deeply humane, to be compassionate and caring, strong and sensitive, to tend to the Garden and watch over the animals. I created Adam and Eve to perfectly fit together as a puzzle, to complete each other in love and to create families in order to love one another and help each other through good times and bad.

All that I created was good.

The Father and I, with Our Holy Spirit, created the heavens and the Earth out of a void. We filled the void with the most beautiful and enlightened creation. We moved on the face of the waters. We created light. We divided the light from the darkness, creating day and night. We divided the waters to create the heavens and oceans on the Earth. We created the land, and it was good. We brought forth trees and vegetation. We created animals and sea creatures of every kind, and it was good. What We created was and is good.

When We created man and woman, We wanted them to have a sense of self. We created them with a will. We created them in Our image and wanted them to enjoy the creation and also create many exquisite works as they lived on the Earth. But many of these works went sour. So much evil would be done over centuries of time. We knew that man and woman had the ability to sin. We knew they would, so We created a plan from the very beginning of time to absolve sin and make a way back to the Garden.

Me.

I was the plan. Not a doctrine. Not a religion. Not a path that is difficult to understand. No. Our plan, the plan of *Elohim*, the first name of God presented in the bible—the Creator, the God in One, was to send Me, Jesus, to Earth in the form of a man at an exact time and place, prophesied through prophets throughout thousands of years, weaving a scarlet thread of redemption for the fall of humanity.

At this specific moment in history—My death on the cross—would become the scapegoat for all sin. Just as the lamb had to be slaughtered in the temple, I had to be slaughtered for humankind. I took the wrath on Myself, because I was God and was with God in the creation. I, the Messiah took the place of judgment for My human beings, because of...

Love.

Love kept Me nailed to the cross. Not power. I had all power. I could have swallowed up the Earth, just as I created it. I could have destroyed it. I could have sent a great fire from heaven and devoured everyone who stood near Me at the crucifixion. Fear did not keep Me nailed to the tree. I had no fear of man. I had no fear of My Father. My devotion to Him did not come out of submission due to fear. It came out of obedience, because in Our plan, there was *no other way.*

I had pleaded with Him in the Garden. "If there is *any* other way... please let this cup pass from Me," but even as I prayed, I knew there was *no* other way.

I was the designated Way. Me. Now. Here. Forsaken. Lonely. Desecrated. The Way, the Truth, and the Life. Me, a person, *Yahuweh* in human form. Forever the face and heart of God. The Messiah, the personal, pivotal, poignant mystery of *Yahuweh.*

Sh'ma Yis'ra'eil Adonai Eloheinu Adonai echad.

Hear, Israel, the Lord is our God, the Lord is One. One God who created the heavens and Earth, who sent His Son to die on the cross—for you.

Darkness covered the Earth, because darkness comes in when the Father is out. God the Father had to separate Himself from the cross, because the sin of humanity was so ugly. And does it not need to be so? Would you want a God who is not righteous, holy and pure?

What sets *Yahuweh* apart from every other god is the personal sacrifice made out of love. It was for the love of the whole world that *Yahuweh* sent Himself, in the form of Jesus, to die for His people. People over thousands of years will talk about energy and molecules colliding in random occurrences, creating big bangs, something out of nothing, but the truth is, My molecules are not colliding in space in a random pattern. My creation is one of perfect order to a perfect plan of redemption that is historically recorded in a timeline of events and in the stars so that anyone who wants to find *Yahuweh*, the Redeemer, can find Him. Anytime, anywhere, anyone who calls on My name, Jesus, he or she is Mine.

As I labored to keep breathing until the redemptive work of the cross was completed, I was thinking of each man, woman or child who has or ever will inhabit the planet Earth.

As I looked inward, to find the place of Love for humanity, to keep my vision so that I would not perish, feeling completely lost and forsaken in the darkness that surrounded Me, as I experienced this momentary separation from God, the Father—I set my face like a flint. I kept my focus on *you*,...

For I was thinking of you, as I am thinking of you now...

When you feel forsaken and lost, when darkness surrounds you, I am with you forever, because I love you.

Setting...
Golgatha

"Eli, Eli, lema sabachthani?"

The thick blanket of darkness had been covering the Earth for almost three hours now. Some thought I called for Elijah, the prophet who was swept up to heaven on a chariot of fire. The people knew that Elijah was with God and wondered if I felt he would come and save Me. These people did not know that when I called for *Eli*, it was for My Father alone.

While I physiologically endured this catastrophic and ultimately terminal event, the worst part of all was the loneliness. No one was with Me. One day, when you walk in your deep valley of loneliness, even in the valley of the shadow of death, or in the place no one in your life understands—it is then, I will be with you. You may endure times of great loneliness to the point where your heart breaks. In those times, I will be with you. I am enduring this loneliness and separation from My Father today, so that I can be with you forever.

My heart, at the point of breaking, held your heart in Mine as I remained suspended in a position that would be difficult even for a contortionist. Now, in a state of hypoventilation, My blood oxygen level fell to the point of hypoxia—low blood oxygen. Because of My restricted respiratory movements, My blood carbon dioxide level began to rise. Hypercapnia stimulated My heartbeat faster in order to increase the oxygen flow to My blood.

My lungs involuntarily struggled to breathe faster. I panted like a dog, heaving in and out as fast as I could. I understood all the functions of a body. I had created the body, but this could not keep the agonizing affliction from reaching levels of insanity. When the body is suffering, the mind can play evil tricks on the soul.

Questions can arise from physical suffering to flood the psyche with doubts. Like in a tsunami, where a series of gigantic waves caused by the displacement of a large volume of water hits the coast with devastating destruction, physical pain wears down the brain and allows a tsunami of doubt to hit the human thoughts over and over and over. Once sane thoughts now begin to become corroded and confused. The mind's stability fatigued by the pain, deteriorates, drowning under the weight of the relentless waves of suffering. Normal rationale is swept away by each overwhelming wave.

The foundations of one's beliefs and understanding are struck by these tidal waves of physical pain, until the very structure of one's faith in all that is good, begins to crumble. When a person undergoes torture or great physical trauma, such as the dismemberment of the body, it is minuscule compared to the dismemberment of the mind. Piece by piece, the mind chafes apart what was integral and whole. Just as village is destroyed by the wave, rational thoughts become a mess of debris bumping into each other, tangling around one another, some hiding in caves, to compartmentalize, in order to make sense of the destruction.

New thoughts emerge—

"Does God love me? Why is this happening to me? What did I do to deserve this pain, this suffering, this torture? How can anyone be so cruel? Why does God allow suffering?" The mind cries out during distress with questions that cannot be answered in the finite walls of time and space.

Torture is about reprogramming the victim to succumb to an alternative exegesis of the world, proffered by the abuser. It is an act of deep, indelible, traumatic indoctrination. Torture is a doubled-edged sword that can harm not only the victim but the perpetrators as well. Many people who torture others have various psychological deviations and often they derive sadistic satisfaction from it. For a considerable degree, torture fulfills the emotional needs of the perpetrator when they willingly engage in these activities. They lack empathy, and their victim's agonized, painful reactions, such as screaming and pleading, give them a sense of authority and feelings of superiority.

As I was being tortured through the crucifixion, I was aware of the evil one who was indeed the one torturing Me. It was none other than satan himself. This would be his last hurrah. He knew he would not triumph. Just as he tempted Me in the Judaean desert after My forty-day fast, he again tried to tempt Me now, through the jeers of the crowd, led by the

212

Sanhedrin's, as they howled in My darkest hour, "If You are the Christ, the King of the Jews, save yourself!"

These cries again echoed satan's words as he had first tempted Me in the wilderness. The first temptation was in reference to My body's base needs, because he knew I had not eaten or had drunk liquid for forty days, and so he attacked My hunger first. "If you are the Son of God, tell these stones to become bread."

Because the spirit is stronger during a fast, I was able to answer,

"Man shall not live by great alone,
But on every word that comes from the mouth of God."

Luke 4:4

This Word is the flaming double-edged sword that can burn up any dart the enemy can throw, but during physical suffering, the mind has a harder time keeping the helmet of salvation in place.

Next he tempted My relationship with God, the Father. He took Me to the pinnacle of the temple in Jerusalem. "If you are the Son of God, throw yourself down, for it is written: 'He will command His angels concerning You, and they will lift You up in their hands so that You will not strike Your foot against a stone.'"

I answered him,

"Do not put the Lord your God to the test."

Now completely desperate, he took Me to a high mountain and showed Me all of the kingdoms of the world and their splendor. "All this I give You," he said, "if You will bow down and worship me."

I commanded him to leave Me,

"Get behind Me, satan, for it is written:
'Worship the Lord your God, and serve Him only.'" *Luke 4:8*

Satan left Me at that point. The Lord sent angels to minister to Me. How I wish those angels could minister to Me now. But there was nothing but darkness and torture for Me now as I continued the arduous task of salvation. I did not relent to satan's temptations in the wilderness, and I would not relent to his temptations now. Yet, even as My thoughts remained steady, as My body writhed in pain, My mind reeled with thoughts... Should I curse the Father? Should I save Myself? What I believed in, is it true?... Was it all true? I am sure the crowd loved this spectacle.

My mind of a man battled thoughts just as you battle thoughts when you are teetering on a tightrope between fear and faith—when satan has worn you down with doubt and confusion, and affliction.

I recalled the words of Psalm 69,

"Save me, O God, for the waters have come up to my neck.

I sink in miry depths, where there is no foothold.

I have come into the deep waters; the floods engulf me."

My heart beat faster and faster as I developed tachycardia. My pulse rate was probably two hundred and twenty beats per minute compared to a normal heart rate of eighty beats per minute.

I had not eaten or drunk anything for twenty hours. I was severely dehydrated. As it was prophesied,

"My throat is parched. My eyes fail, looking for God.

Those that hate me without reason outnumber the hairs of my head;

Many are my enemies without cause, those who seek to destroy me.

I am forced to restore, what I did not steal." Psalm 69:4

When they offered Me wine to drink, mixed with myrrh, I did not drink it, so as to fulfill My words at the last supper when I said to My disciples, "I will never again drink of the fruit of the vine until that day when I drink it anew in the kingdom of God."

"How I am scorned, disgraced and shamed.

Scorn has broken my heart and has left me helpless.

I looked for sympathy, but there was none. For comforters, I found none.

They put gall in my food and gave me vinegar for my thirst."

Psalm 69:20-21

My blood pressure dropped extremely low. Lack of oxygen to My brain was causing dizziness, fainting and nausea. I was now in first degree shock, and My heart began to fail. My lungs were filling up with *pulmonary oedema*—fluid accumulation in the air spaces and substance of My lungs. This will eventually lead to more respiratory distress and cardiac arrest due to hypoxia.

To save My life at this point, I would have needed to be lifted off of this cross, My wounds sealed up, wrapped in warm blankets, and have an intravenous infusion of blood and plasma. But My body would not be saved this day. My blood and water would be poured out for you, for I was thinking of you, as I am thinking of you now...

214

As I was suffocating and developing hemopericardium, where plasma and blood gathered in the space around My heart, called the pericardium, and before I would cry out for the last time, I thought of all of the martyrs that would be tortured, burned at the stake, and hung on crosses. I thought of My beloved Peter who would ask to be hung upside down on his cross, not even feel worthy to identify with Me in his death.

I thought of the precious ones whose blood would lay the foundations of the church. I thought of those who will have faith as they are stoned, sawn in two, tempted, and put to death with the sword. I thought of those who will go about in sheep skins, in goatskins, being destitute, afflicted, and ill-treated—men and women of whom the world is not worthy—those who will wander in deserts, mountains, caves and holes in the ground, not receiving their promise on Earth, but looking for a better place, a heavenly home. I will not be ashamed to be called their God, for I have prepared a city for them. *Hebrews 11*

"They will not come to a mountain that can be touched and burned with
fire. Those who come to Me will come to Mount Zion,
The city of the living God, the heavenly Jerusalem.
They will come to thousands upon thousands of angels who gather in joy."
Hebrews 12:18,22

"They will come to God, the judge of all, to the spirits of the
Righteous made perfect, and to Me, Jesus,
The mediator of the new covenant..."
Hebrews 12:23,24

Those who die for Me and those who live for Me will receive an unshakable kingdom, which cannot be moved.

It will not be without price. It will not be without My price that I pay today. And it will not be without the price of the blood of martyrs who carry My torch to offer freedom and justice to all those oppressed.

As I am about to breathe My last breath, I am conscious of all those who will go after Me in My name who will have the same questions that flooded My mind as I endured the cross.

"Eli, Eli, lama sabachthani?"

My God, My God—Why have You forsaken Me?

Every Christian martyr will feel endure similar thoughts as I have today. Those who die without receiving the promises, those whom the world is not worthy of—will know that the world was not worthy of their Messiah either.

Thousands of Christians will die in the first century of the church. Hundreds of thousands of martyrs will die throughout thousands of years after that, and will continue to do so until I come again...

"These all died in faith, not having received the promises,
But having seen them afar off, and were persuaded of them,
And embraced them, and confessed that they were strangers and pilgrims
On the earth.
For they that say such things declare plainly that they seek a country.
And truly, if they had been mindful of that country from whence they came
out, they might have had opportunity to have returned.
But now they desire a better country, that is, a heavenly one:
Wherefore God is not ashamed to be called their God:
For he hath prepared for them a city."
Hebrews 11:13-16

I have prayed for them, and for you. With the very incense of My body, I have offered up a sacrifice, so that when you are in your darkest moments, *I am with* you. I have paved a way for you. Where I go, you will be with Me, for I am thinking of you.

Remember, the Earth is not your home.

Your home is in Me.

216

Setting...
Golgatha

John 19:28-30

"I am thirsty."

When I spoke these words, there is no way I could describe the complete lack of hydration that I felt in My body. Here I was, the Living Water, who came to give life to the world, and I could not feel an ounce of liquid to quench the burning fire in my mouth, my tongue, nor my lungs. My body's fluids were at a level where most people would have already been dead. The fluid levels around My heart were at a point of panic. I was close to having a heart attack.

The announcement of My thirst to the crowd was not to receive the sour wine that the soldier offered Me. Whether he was moved with compassion or mockery, no, the drink was not to quench My thirst. I said these words to express the finality of the separation between Myself and the Father at that point. Being God in man, I had never once mentioned My needs during My ministry on Earth. I did not mention them when I was a boy either. I had no need to. My mother attended to My every need, and I was an obedient child with no need to be punished. My earthly father, Joseph, treated Me fairly, with compassion and provided for Me. My Father in heaven looked out for Me spiritually, emotionally and mentally.

I had only thought of others during the time of My anointed journey on Earth. I had no place to lay My head. I possessed no earthly possessions. I did not own a house or acquire livestock. I did not live to achieve a goal of affluence. I had one mission—to walk on the Earth, to feel what My created beings felt, to join them in their arduous journey, to experience their pain, and to take their sins on My back—to drink the cup of My Father's will, and to die on the cross of My Father's choice.

Today I thirst, but tomorrow people will drink of Me, the *Mayim Hayim,* the Living Water.

I recalled again when I stood up before the people in the temple on the Feast of *Sukkot*, the Feast of Tabernacles, which is an eight-day festival. The first and the eighth days are special days of rest, set apart from the others. The seventh day is known as *Hoshana Rabba*, "The Great Day." During this day, there is a water ceremony. The worshippers and flutists, led by the priest, visit the pool of Siloam, the same pool where I had put clay in the blind man's eyes, told him to wash in the pool, and his sight was restored.

At the water ceremony of *Sukkot*, the priest carries two golden pitchers. One is filled with wine. The other one he dips into the pool and fills it with water. A trumpet sounds as they return through the Water Gate to the temple. Here the priest approaches two silver basins. He pours the wine as a drink offering to the Lord into one and the water from the pool into the other. This joyful ceremony is to thank God for His bounty and to ask Him to provide rain for another year of crops.

It was at this festival I arose in the crowd of My peers only three years ago—people I had grown up with—people I had had fellowship with in the temple since My youth. I had proclaimed the opposite of what I cried out today. I said,

"If anyone thirsts, let him come to Me and drink. He who believes in Me,
As the scripture has said, out of his belly, his inner being,
His heart will flow rivers of living water.'" John 7:37

The *Mayim Hayim,* Me, the Messiah, the One for whom they had been waiting, standing in the middle of the festival, stretched out My arms to the people to welcome Me as their Messiah. The image of Me, stretching out My hands nailed to a cross, displayed a stark contrast to that day.

The symbols of the festival are water and light. Later I proclaimed,

"I am the Light of the world.
He who follows Me will never walk in darkness, but have the light of life."
John 8:12

The temple was filled with candles during the feast.

The sky over Jerusalem glowed from these golden lamps shining from the temple set on a hill. In addition to the light, Levitical musicians played their harps, lyres, cymbals and trumpets to make joyful music to the Lord. What a glorious celebration!

The light was to remind the people of how God's *Shekinah* glory had once filled His temple, the same glory which now shown in Me. It was in the court of women just after the Feast, standing next to those magnificent candelabras, that I declared I was the Light of the world.

How different I appeared today, with the dismal tenebrosity that draped the sky, framing Me in a shroud of gloom. I did not look like the Savior of the world, yet it is in this act, as My heart is breaking in two, I am pouring out My water, and with it My blood, fulfilling the two golden pitchers of *Sukkot*.

My light is an eternal flame that cannot be put out. One day, when there will be no more sun, there will be no need for the sun. I will be the Light of New Jerusalem.

As I thirst, I remain focused on those who believe in Me and never thirst again.

I will not be with you much longer in My flesh. Because of the physiological events of My body putting strain upon My heart.

My heart is breaking...

The bursting of My heart will be the symbol of a God who loved the world so much that He gave His only Son.

Even as I open this door to eternal life, I am sad to leave My followers, My mother, and My friends. It grieves Me so, that I cannot be with them anymore in My body. But I go to another place, and I will receive them again with Me, but more importantly, I will be with them always, in the Spirit.

Conquering death on the cross, I am completely victorious over the enemies of their soul and of yours. Darkness has no more power over My people. The people who call upon My name will be freed forever. The Truth will set them free.

"If the Son sets you free, you will be free indeed." John 8:36

When you feel tormented by satan, when he and his deceitful fallen angels are lying to you, causing you to feel insane, confused, or afraid, you will know that I have overcome them. Today the head of the lying serpent is crushed forever. In My death is the glory, the power, and the kingdom forever.

As I finished the work on the cross, I was thinking of you, as I am thinking of you now...

Cardiac rupture is upon Me now.

At three in the afternoon, I shouted with a cry that came from deep within My bowels—

219

"Tetelastai."

"It is finished."

The questions that had swirled around My head, "Maybe We expected too much out of humankind? Are We at fault? Is the God who created the heavens and the earth at fault for creating human beings to have fellowship with, meanwhile giving them a free will to choose?"

Even in creation, knowing there would be evil on the earth, We created the way out of the circle of sin. Can you find any fault with God's perfect plan and in the perfect unblemished Lamb of God?

We thought that, with the ethereal world We created, and with the perfect beauty in which We created it, humankind would be happy and good forever.

These questions I had were nailed to the cross with Me.

I was the Answer.

Sadness...

Sadness was nailed to Me on the cross.

Sin...

Sin was nailed to Me on the cross.

Death...

Death was nailed to Me on the cross.

Every fear, hurt, grief, sickness, sin or death, was nailed to Me.

When you are in your worst hour of catastrophe, when you face fear, grief, sickness and death, I am with you, for I was thinking of you, as I am thinking of you now...

As I cried out with the voice of many waters, the Earth began to quake. The shaking of the Earth was nothing compared to the shaking of My eternal and final work in breaking My heart to become the Temple of God. The souls, who call on Me, freed for now and eternity, I could hear in My spirit. I could hear them rejoicing with hope as the thick veil that separated them from intimate fellowship with God—ripped open like the day the waters parted in two at the Red Sea. When the children of Israel, once slaves, were freed, passed out of Egypt, walked on dry ground through the sea to the promised land. The waters stood still at the command of *Yahuweh.*

Today, the Holy of Holies was accessible to anyone who receives His plan of salvation—*No more separation from God.*

220

Here on the fourteenth day of Nisan, I, the unblemished Lamb, was slaughtered. My blood, now poured over the door of the hearts of those who believe in Me, will be the exodus from the bondage of sin to the promised land of peace and rest.

When God required a perfect sacrifice, the rows of priests with gold or silver cups in their hands, stood in line from the temple courts to the altar where the blood was sprinkled. These cups were rounded on the bottom so that they could not be set down, for if they did, the blood might coagulate.

The priest caught the blood as it dropped from the lamb, then handed the cup to the priest next to him, receiving from him an empty one. The cup was passed along the line until it reached the last priest, who sprinkled its contents on the altar.

As the sacrificial Lamb, My heart ripped apart, opened the door into the inner room—called the Holy of Holies, the most sacred room, where no ordinary person could enter. The veil, a divider that hid the Glory of God from man, which separated sinful humanity from the presence of God, ripped from top to bottom. The beautiful veil was made of fine linen with blue, purple and scarlet yarn. Intricately embroidered onto the veil were figures of cherubim—the angels who were spoken of by Ezekiel, with eyes all around, with a head of a man, a lion, an eagle, and a cherub—the cherubim who serve God, surround Him night and day, and guard the throne of God.

Before this moment, only the high priest, God's chosen mediator, could pass through the veil one day a year on the Day or Atonement. Even this priest had to make meticulous preparations to enter the Holy of Holies. He had to wash himself, put on special clothing, prepare burning incense which he brought before him as a smoke cover to shield his eyes from a direct view of God. And most importantly, he had to bring a perfect blood sacrifice.

As the Earth rumbled, the hand of *Yahuweh*, Himself, seized the veil, sixty feet high, thirty feet wide and four inches thick, and tore it from top to bottom. My work on the cross was complete. My Father had accepted My obedient and perfect sacrifice.

As the veil split, the earth quaked, rocks split in two and tombs were opened. I conquered death. Death had no sting. My death came by My hand, by My will, by My plan, by My surrendering of My power, by

221

My last and final breath, given up of My own free will—the ultimate offering had been sacrificed. I had tasted death for all men, women and children.

Therefore, have confidence. You can enter the most holy place of *Yahuweh* by My blood. You can draw near to God with a sincere heart and with full assurance of faith, for I was thinking of you, as I am thinking of you now....

My last thought was of you, as I cried with a loud voice...

"Father, into your hands, I commit My spirit."

"When the centurion and those who were guarding Jesus saw
The earthquake and all that happened, they were terrified,
And exclaimed,
"Surely, he was the Son of God!"
The centurion glorified God, saying, certainly this was
A righteous man. All the people that came together to watch
The crucifixion, having seen these things, smote their breasts."
Matthew 27:54

Eve's Memoirs and other books

& art by Lauri Matisse available at:

www.EvesMemoirs.com

www.LauriMatisse.com

www.mystikcenter.com

Lauri's Blog: *Weaving Light*

LauriMatisseBlog.wordpress.com

For information on Eve The Musical:

contact LauriMatisse@gmail.com

End Times Info:

www.mystikcenter.com

https://livingwatersoflife.wixsite.com/nebraskapreppers

www.calculatingthelastseven.com

Support the work of translating this book into other languages:

https://www.patreon.com/LauriMatisse

Made in the USA
Monee, IL
22 February 2020

22100543R00125